I0083384

PROCESS FOR PURPOSE

Learning to Trust God's Plan and Purpose in Your Season of Waiting

Sherine Leslie-Gooden

PROCESS FOR PURPOSE. Copyright © 2024. Sherine Leslie-Gooden. All Rights Reserved.

Printed in the United States of America.

No portion of this book may be reproduced, stored in a retrieval system, or transmitted in any form or by any means, except for brief quotations in printed reviews, without the prior written permission of DayeLight Publishers or Sherine Leslie-Gooden.

DAYELight
PUBLISHERS

ISBN: 978-1-958443-59-0 (paperback)

There are two scriptures that I use to keep me going each day. Even when I can't make sense of all that is happening in my life, I know God knows.

Romans 8:28 - And we know that all things work together for good to them that love God, to them who are the called according to his purpose. (KJV).

Jeremiah 29:11 - For I know the thoughts that I think toward you, saith the LORD, thoughts of peace, and not of evil, to give you an expected end. (KJV).

Dedication

This book is dedicated to all those who are in their season of processing and are feeling weary and hopeless. You may be wondering where God is; He is right there with you. My prayer is that this book will give you the strength and encouragement you need to go through your process in order to reach the next level God has for you.

This book is also dedicated to my husband, Clive, and my daughter, Gianna. My husband is my number one fan and cheerleader. I truly appreciate you and thank God for you. My daughter, Gianna, is one of the greatest gifts I have received from God. Thank you both for the love and joy you bring to my heart and life.

Acknowledgments

I want to extend my heartfelt gratitude to God, my heavenly Father, who placed within me the desire to see lives transformed through His Word. To Him be all the glory and honour.

To my husband, Clive, for always encouraging and supporting me.

To my sister, Sheredine, for always encouraging me.

Thanks to all my friends and family who have been praying for me.

May God continue to bless you all.

Table of Contents

Table of Contents

Introduction

Proverbs 3:5-6 - Trust in the Lord with all thine heart; and lean not unto thine own understanding. In all thy ways acknowledge him, and he shall direct thy paths. (KJV).

For many, processing can mean several things. A process is a series of actions or steps taken to achieve a particular end. There are some things that need to happen in our lives before we can step into what God has for us. We all must go through spiritual processing in order to be the great men and women God calls us to be.

Depending on your submission to the Holy Spirit, some processes will take longer than others. It is never easy when we are stripped of certain old habits; we become uncomfortable with change because we are so used to doing things a particular way. Many of us have found ourselves in a dark place. I must say that I haven't always handled that place very well. This process can sometimes be very painful because we are confronted with issues that we don't want to deal with. The process is like a diamond in the refinery process, created by extremely high temperatures and heat, but on the inside of it lies something beautiful. God wants us to be processed in order to bring forth that purpose on the inside of us.

We are selfish and self-centered by nature, and that is not how it works in the kingdom of God. We must esteem others above ourselves. In the world we are living in today, it is "Me first and everyone else after." We are all placed on the face of this earth for a purpose; we weren't born as an accident. We are created for a purpose, and in order to fulfil that purpose, we have to go to the One with the blueprint for our lives.

The definition of the word "process" is a procedure; something you do in order to achieve a certain result. For us to be like Christ, in terms of His character, we have to be processed. God is not going to send us to do great things unless He knows we are able to handle all the success that comes with it. We tend to allow the process to affect us in such a way that we forget that He is the reason why we are. As for me, my processing brought up a lot that was within me that I didn't know was there, both good and bad.

Sometimes we are full of unforgiveness, hatred, anger, jealousy, envy, malice, and strife. God cannot use us if we are not set free from these spirits. We must go through a deliverance process to move forward to the place God wants to take us. God's business has a lot to do with people, and people are called to love people. If we are not delivered from these spirits, we won't be able to help those who are hurting and in need of our help. Have you ever heard the saying, "Hurting people hurt people?"

The second command given by God is to love our neighbour as we love ourselves (see Matthew 22:39). How are you going to love your neighbour if you don't know how to love yourself? There is a seed of greatness inside you, and there are people out there waiting on you to deliver them from what they are going through. I have learned that in order to reach where God intended for me to reach, I had to yield, trust, and wait during the process. While those days felt unbearable, I learned that my peace and joy come when I cry out to God and release all my cares to Him. I have learned that if God allowed it to happen, He has a purpose for it.

Are there any deep hurts and disappointments in your life that seem to be lingering? Have you prayed the same prayers repeatedly with little to no change? I understand how you feel and how hard that is. Over the last few years, I have walked through some of the most heartbreaking seasons in my finances, marriage, family, and health.

My process may be totally different from the things you had to endure, but it was still your process. You probably have moments where you cry yourself to sleep. The process often requires us to be patient and, maybe, even long-suffering. Honestly, I know that can feel a little overwhelming. Trust the process; keep praying, hoping, and cry out to Him. The process will not kill you; it will only make you stronger.

Chapter 1

When Crises Comes Knocking

Why, God?

Have you ever asked God, "Why?" I have! If we are honest, we probably asked or thought about that question at some point in our lives, especially under extreme pain or pressure.

"God, why did You let me go through this painful situation? Did I do something wrong? Why do bad things happen to good people? Why do You feel so far away?" These are questions we ask ourselves at some point in our lives. Life is tough and unpredictable and rarely happens the way we plan. It is hard to understand how a loving God would allow us to experience pain and disgrace. It is not just any pain, but the kind that is a public disgrace and may cost you your integrity and reputation.

On January 27, 2017, I was arrested by the police at my office. I experienced fear, and many questions dominated my mind, but one question was more paralyzing and difficult to answer: *"Why me, Lord?"* I was detained at the Duhaney Park Police Station for seven days along with three of my coworkers. We were held for questioning by the police because it was alleged that we were committing fraud at work. Everything happened so fast that the officers took me to my home where they searched for evidence to tie me to something that I didn't do. They searched and didn't find anything. They confiscated my passport, laptop, cell phone, and the documents for my house. I was taken to jail, where I spent one week sleeping on concrete with newspaper as my sheet. Four of us were in one cell with no proper bathroom facilities. While there, we weren't allowed any visitors; they could only leave whatever items they brought for us at the front desk.

It was a very terrifying experience. I felt like I was about to lose my mind. That week felt like my whole world had shut down, and God was silent. I felt like Job that day. I was saved, so why would God allow that to happen to me? I was a person of integrity, so *how did this happen?* Deep down in my spirit, I felt an assurance that God was going to take me through that traumatic experience. I had to rely on Him for strength, and I was trying to be strong for the others who were in the same situation as I was.

I have gone through traumatic experiences before, such as losing my mother at the age of sixteen. She was my motivator and encouragement. It was heartbreaking, but God brought me through. Yet, being arrested shocked me to the core, especially because I was not guilty of the

16

accusations being brought against me. That was a different kind of pain.

As the week progressed—still in jail and as broken as I was—I had to lean into the Lord for strength and comfort. Even with the fear and doubt running through my mind, I started to gain strength as I meditated and read the Word of God. I kept hearing Romans 8:28 playing in my mind along with Travis Green's song "You Made Away." I read the scripture, but I just couldn't see how it was going to work out for me at the time.

While in jail, I read the entire book of Job within a day. He had lost everything, yet he refused to curse God, even when his wife was telling him to do so. I started to see my situation as a Job experience. Just like Job, the very thing I feared happened to me because of the nature of my job. I stood on the fact that God gave Job double for his trouble, and He would do the same for me. Even though what I was seeing on the surface didn't look pretty at all, I was reminded by 2 Corinthians 5:7 that we walk by faith and not by sight, and Romans 8:28 that all things work together for good.

It was the worst week of my entire life. I felt like I was in hell; it was a very long week. Even so, praise and worship was still coming out of my spirit. The girls and I kept prayer meetings, sang songs, read the Bible, and played games at night just to keep our minds at peace. I would find myself encouraging the other girls from the different cells in the prison and keeping prayer meetings with them. By doing so, I found encouragement myself.

Finally, Friday came for us to go to court. It felt like it took forever to come. We were escorted to the court, where we were granted bail; however, it was too late for the bail completion process. We were then taken to Fort Augusta Adult Correctional Center, which was located in Portmore, St. Catherine at the time. We spent the weekend there. It was much better than sleeping on the concrete with newspaper, but it was another terrifying weekend for me. I had to continue to rest in the promises of God's Word, knowing that despite how it may look, it was going to work out for my good. I don't know how or when, but that was the word God placed in my spirit.

I felt scared because of the behaviour of some of the other ladies there. I was not accustomed to that type of violent behaviour. I have never anticipated Monday like that in my life. It was a more terrifying experience than being at the other lockup. The environment was so tense, toxic, miserable, and lacking in the presence of God. With the help and strength of God, I survived the weekend.

Thank God, Monday was finally here, and I was eagerly awaiting my release. I was so anxious that I couldn't sit still that morning. It was in the afternoon before one of the officers came to let me know that it was time for me to go. I grabbed my things and ran as if I were running from someone or running for my life. She took me back to the

Halfway Tree Courthouse, where I was granted my bail release and was on conditional bail. I was to return to court on February 6, 2017, and report to the Rockfort Police Station every Monday between the hours of 6 am and 6 pm. I was placed on interdiction with just a quarter of my salary and couldn't work another job because of the nature of the case and the fact that I was still employed to the company. Most of my quarter pay was used to pay my mortgage and other deductions, and whatever was left over would be sent to my account. It was that same January 2017 when I got my first salary increase, and all of that was out the door.

Fear And Worry

I became so fearful to the point where I didn't like to see Fridays because my mind would go back to that morning when I was arrested. I would fear going to court because I kept thinking they would send me back to prison or back to that horrible jail cell. I was fearful of the fact that I was going to go to prison for something I didn't do. God wasn't answering my prayers for the person or persons who were involved to confess what they had done so the innocent could be freed.

It is easy to panic in the midst of our circumstances as the disciples did on the boat. We tend to forget who is by our side and assume the absolute worst. Yes, I held on to my faith, but I was so fearful of the unknown. I was worried about how I was going to repay my loan and other expenses.

I was worried about what the future might hold for me, and that created anxiety and stress.

I was so caught up in knowing why this situation happened to me that I couldn't see the good that was to come from it. After all, I was a person of integrity; I am honest and trustworthy. It didn't seem fair that God would allow such a thing to happen to me while I was serving Him. Then, I reflected on what Job went through being a man of integrity himself, but I couldn't accept the fact that it was going to work out for my good with my reputation being ruined publicly.

Every day I would replay everything in my head leading up to that day, and I kept asking myself, "Where did I go wrong?" I was as alert as I could be in my environment, so how did I not see this coming? I had to also adjust to not being able to work, which was hard for me. I was not used to staying home and not doing anything. I had been working since I left high school, so it was hard for me to comprehend at that time.

Change Your Posture

One day, while laying down worrying, I felt strong in my spirit that God was telling me to take my eyes off the situation and focus on Him. I felt a sense of peace. I realize that I was trying to win the case in my own strength, but God shifted my perspective. I sensed the Spirit of God saying the question I needed to ask was not "Why?" but "What do You want me to learn from this journey? What good do You want to bring from this? What testimony will You bring from this?" Even though my "why" wasn't answered, I started to see answers to my "what" questions. I started to get deeper in my faith by building a personal relationship with God. It was then that I realized He was moulding me into a strong woman of faith. He wanted me to trust Him like never before.

It is not always easy being moulded, and the process requires a mindset shift. You must make an intentional decision, act and trust that God wants to bring something good out of your situation, and that it is for your ultimate good. Then we will be able to impact others with what we have been through and the lessons we have learned.

I was going through my journal one day, and I saw a prayer that I had written asking God to provide me with another job. I wanted to leave the place where I was working because of various situations. There and then, I sensed the Holy Spirit saying to me, "Sometimes God answers your prayers but not in the way you are expecting Him to. Sometimes you must be pushed out of your comfort zone or you will never grow to your full potential." I honestly didn't look at my situation like that until I came across the prayer and the sensing of the Holy Spirit. Even though it was embarrassing and painful, God may have allowed it, just like with Job, to get me to where He wanted to take me. He wanted me to get to that place where I understood the purpose and plans He had for my life.

Instead of getting up in the morning with worry and fear, I started to dwell more on the Word of God. I used my energy to pray, worship, watch preaching on YouTube, meditate, and dwell in the Word of God. I realized that each day, I was beginning to have a different perspective about my situation. I was looking at my situation from God's perspective and not mine. I was no longer just seeing in the natural. It wasn't easy, and I had to choose whether to be fearful and worry or trust the Word of God every day. What we focus on will magnify. I must be intentional everyday about not keeping my eyes on my situation, but to build my relationship with God and yield to my process daily.

We can't always change our circumstances, but with God's help, we can change our thoughts and attitudes towards what we are facing. We must guard our hearts in order to change our thoughts. This will protect us from the doubt and fear we are wrestling with, and that will help us stand firm and fight against the wiles of the devil. Instead of waking up each day feeling defeated, wake up every morning feeling victorious. Instead of saying, "I am not going to come out of this situation," tell yourself that you are coming out strong because the God you serve is bigger than the circumstance.

Speak with faith. Keep expecting and start praising God before the breakthrough comes. Keep speaking to your situation. Cry out and surrender all to God. Surround yourself with people stronger than you in faith. Do not be afraid to ask for prayer and get into the Word of God because that is where all the answers to your problems are. Meditate on the Word of God daily. Build a personal relationship with God and keep your eyes on Him.

It is easy to be thankful and praise God when things are going well in our life, but when something goes wrong, that is usually where all the praises stop. We struggle to see God as being good anymore, so we tend to give up on Him. We need to remember that we are not our own; we belong to Jesus. He ordained the plan for our lives, and He knows what is best for us. We need to change our attitude and posture as to how we perceive our circumstances.

God would not permit the storm if He didn't place enough in you to go through it. There are days when I wanted to throw in the towel, but I couldn't find the strength to do so. Instead, I gained more strength to go on. God would place a word or a song in my spirit that would minister to me for the entire day. The devil must get permission from God before he can put a storm in your life. God must approve it first. I know you might be wondering, "Why do Godly people suffer? Why does God allow undeserved suffering?" Yes, I too have asked those questions many times.

Sometimes the, unfortunate circumstances are allowed to build your character, to mould you and make you into the person God wants you to be. The storms will keep some of us on our knees; they will provoke us to read our Bibles and go to church on a regular basis. Based on my experience, God did not permit the storm to kill us but to make us more like Him. Jesus went through His fair share of storms while here on earth, yet He didn't yield to the pressure.

We can choose to surrender and move forward with God or stay stuck in our pain and disappointments. You can get through any circumstance in life, if you choose to face it with faith in God. Worrying robs us of happiness and valuable opportunities for growth and development. Worrying, fear, and anxiety are just a waste of your energy. They get you nowhere; they seldom produce any solution to your situation.

Maybe you can relate somehow to my story. It could be that you have gone through a divorce, a bad report from the doctor, loss of a job, or a miscarriage. When we expect things to get better and they don't, it can leave us with a lot of questions. It is not wrong to ask God questions and express our emotions. David, Job, and even Jesus felt like they had been abandoned by God. God already knows what we are going through and how we feel, and He wants us to express ourselves to Him.

At the writing of this book, the court matter had been drawn out for seven years. That is a long time to wait.

My brethren, count it all joy when ye fall into divers temptations; Knowing this, that the trying of your faith worketh patience. But let patience have her perfect work, that ye may be perfect and entire, wanting nothing. (James 1:2-4 – KJV).

24

As 2023 comes to a close, the case didn't end the way I expected, but I am still trusting that God will work it out for my good and for His glory in His perfect timing.

Chapter 2

The Crises Keeps Knocking

Where Are You, Lord?

In the year 2020, when my daughter was born, the doctor who checked us on the ward was concerned because, according to their expertise, her two middle fontanelles were too wide. It was not the average size for a normal baby.

When I was discharged from the hospital, I was given a referral to have an x-ray done. I ignored that because I didn't feel the conviction in my spirit that something was wrong with my child. I prayed and declared that "It is well" and rested in God.

I took her to the paediatrician for her regular checks and the paediatrician was concerned. I was told to get the x-ray because there may be water in her brain. I felt devastated, so I went and got the test done that same day. The results came back normal. Thanks be to God. After the results came back normal, the paediatrician was still not convinced and sent us to do another blood test to check her thyroid. The results came back negative. It felt like every time we visited, the paediatrician would have more concerns, and God proved her wrong every time. It was a stressful period for my husband and me because she was our first child, and we wanted the best for her. Within a few months, that paediatrician was no longer working there, so we went back to our regular paediatrician, who didn't seem overly concerned or put us through the stress the first one did. To God be all the glory, my daughter is healthy and smart. She continues to exceed our expectations in her stages of development.

In life, you must learn to trust God despite what the doctors are saying. God is the greatest Physician, and He will never leave or forsake us.

In that same year, my husband was battling unknown health issues. He did test after test, and all the results came back normal. I continued to pray, believing and trusting that God would come through for him. Remember, I just had a baby. It was rough because my husband would be the one to relieve me in the evening after he got home from work.

On August 6, 2021, I had to take my daughter to the doctor because she wasn't feeling well. She had trouble breathing the night before. I took her to the paediatrician but I was sent to children's hospital. My daughter spent three days in the hospital because of a viral infection. She was placed on the isolation ward awaiting a COVID-19 test results. I spent the entire day there without anything to eat because of the

COVID-19 protocols; only one parent was allowed in the hospital. The waiting process at the hospital was so long and exhausting, and I was alone with my daughter. The ward she was admitted on didn't accommodate visitors and that was very hard for her and for us as parents. It was a very difficult time.

Even though I wasn't able to be with her physically, I would still go to the hospital and watch her through the window. I cried. It was so heartbreaking to stand at a window looking at her crying and knowing that I was not able to be with her. She had never slept without us before, so it was really hard for her to be away from us. Each day I went by the hospital, my heart would be aching. On the third day of being on the isolation ward, her test came back negative, and I was able to take her home.

At home, my husband, his mother, aunt, and niece contracted the COVID-19 virus. His mother was not able to breathe. She was placed on oxygen and was still having challenges breathing. It was a really rough time for our family. Between August 19 and 22, 2022, my husband lost his mother and aunt to the COVID-19 virus. It was a very hard time for him because he was very close to them.

On August 25, 2022, I felt like I was about to pass out and started to panic. I was at my house in Old Harbour, St. Catherine at the time, and there was no transportation there to take me to the doctor. I thought I was going to die because of how I felt. My whole life flashed before my eyes, and I began to panic even more. My sister ran across to one of our neighbours and he decided to take me to a doctor. All the doctor's offices were full and I would have to wait a long time because of the pandemic and the different restrictions that were enforced. I was panicking even more.

My husband eventually came and took me to a hospital in Kingston. Again, there was a long wait. I waited for hours before I was able to see a doctor because my situation was not seen as a crisis. Finally, I got to see the doctor. I did some tests, and the results revealed that my heart rhythm was irregular at the time and I was having heart palpitations. My D-Dimer blood test was very high, indicating that I had an infection. All the other test results came back negative. I was given a prescription and a referral to see a cardiologist because of the irregular heart rate.

I went to the cardiologist the following week. An echocardiogram was done, and it showed that I had trace tricuspid regurgitation present, which was not considered serious and had nothing to do with what I was experiencing based on the cardiologist's assessment. I was given a holter monitor (portable electrocardiogram) for 24 hours to try and determine what was causing my increased heartrate. I was given instructions to record what I was doing at the time that my heartrate increased. I took the monitor back to the cardiologist the following day and, based on the cardiologist's evaluation, I was experiencing anxiety. He gave me a prescription with a strong dose of heart medication plus xanax for anxiety.

I took the heart medication and it made my situation even worse. There were days I was not able to get out of bed because of the side effects of the medication. I felt like my body had no use. I was weak, dizzy, and lightheaded. My husband had to do everything around the house, including taking care of our daughter and making funeral arrangements for his mom and aunt. It was a very difficult time for my marriage and motherhood; my daughter was only one year old. Thank God for my husband. He stood by me and encouraged me every step of the way, even though he had his own issues dealing with.

I kept praying to and believing God that my health would turn around speedily. Each morning I got up, it felt like the situation was getting worse instead of better. I spent most of my days googling my symptoms and self-diagnosing myself, and I would start to believe that I was suffering from the sicknesses I was reading about. I would then run to the doctor to have the test done and all the tests would come back negative. I was battling health anxiety because of how I was feeling. For months, I would be going back and forth to doctors without getting a diagnosis. It got to a point where my health card was maxed out.

I got so weary and burnt out trying to fix the situation in my own strength. I was at the point where I couldn't pray or read my Bible.

I went to bed one night and had a dream that I went to a doctor, and he told me he couldn't do anything for me because what I was going through was spiritual. I was booked to see a naturopathic doctor the following week, and when I went there, he happened to be a pastor. He told me that what I was going through was spiritual warfare, and he gave me some scriptures to read. That was the same dream I had the week before. The truth is, I heard about spiritual warfare before but didn't know much about it until I experienced it myself. I had to get in an atmosphere that taught about warfare and strategies to fight.

Spiritual Warfare

Ephesians 6:12 - For we wrestle not against flesh and blood, but against principalities, against powers, against the rulers of the darkness of this world, against spiritual wickedness in high places. (KJV).

I became vigilant and learned all I could about spiritual warfare and how to respond to it. Spiritual warfare is real and should be taken seriously. According to Wikipedia, spiritual warfare is the Christian concept of fighting against preternatural evil forces. We must recognise who our true enemy is. There is a real enemy—the devil—out there that is after our souls. His main job is to kill, steal, and destroy what God has placed inside of you. The battleground is your heart and mind, and we must have a strategy to win. We must learn when it is the enemy attacking us and pull on the Word of God. He can attack our health, marriage, career, finances, and even use our children. For me, I was being attacked in more than one way: my job, health, marriage, and child. He also tries to convince you to doubt the Word of God and believe his lies instead.

We must come into the light of the truth of God's Word that brings deliverance from bondage. The Bible said that we will know the truth, and the truth will set us free.

John 8:32 - And you shall know the truth, and the truth shall make you free. (NKJV).

Our family, friends, coworkers, and people are not our enemy; they are the tools used by our real enemy, satan. Whenever persons do us wrong, it is not really the person but the spirit operating through them. He knows that if you ever come to the realization of the purpose and plans God has for you, you will create havoc in his kingdom, so he tries to hold you captive.

It was the truth that set me free from all the lies the enemy was telling me. We are told in Ephesians 6:11 to put on the whole armour of God so we can stand against the enemy of our souls. Use the Word of God daily because it is alive and waiting to give life. Hebrews 4:12 states that the Word of God is quick and powerful and sharper than any two-edged sword. Go to a church that teaches about warfare and believes in deliverance. Some things we are going through cannot be fought in the natural but need spiritual attention.

Through the power of the Holy Spirit, it was later revealed to me by a deliverance minister that the sickness I was

33

experiencing was a witchcraft-inspired sickness and needed divine intervention. God was there with me through it all and was able to show me in a dream what was happening to me. I was fighting my problem naturally; hence, I wasn't getting any results.

You Are The Healed of God

1 Peter 2:24 - who Himself bore our sins in His own body on the tree, that we, having died to sins, might live for righteousness—by whose stripes you were healed. (NKJV).

I was sitting in the living room one morning listening to TBN on the television. Pastor Andrew Wommack was doing a series called "God Wants You Well." I sat there listening when I heard him say, "God wants you well." I said to myself, "If God wants me well, then why am I not healed? I must be doing something wrong." Pastor Wommack quoted 1 Peter 2:24 and said, "You're already healed. It is finished. You have to just take authority and walk in the truth." Right there and then, I received a revelation. I realized that I wasn't praying or walking in my authority of healing because I was begging and pleading with God to heal me, but it was already done. I just needed to take authority. I got a faith injection that day, and my prayer for healing was never the same again. I started to research Andrew Wommack and found his website with a lot of testimonies about persons being healed from terminal illnesses. Instead of googling my symptoms each day, I started to watch those testimonies daily to strengthen my faith.

I continued to soak on healing teachings and testimonies despite the symptoms I was feeling. I continued to believe in God that I was already healed. I know our faith can be easily shaken based on what we are seeing, but I was reminded that we walk by faith and not sight (see 2 Corinthians 5:7).

You may be feeling the symptoms and the pain, but continue to trust God that it is finished. It was my unbelief that was causing me to doubt God, because it wasn't happening on my timetable and because of the symptoms I was still experiencing. Don't give the symptoms any room to remain in your body and cause suffering. Speak out. Take authority given to you by the blood of Christ and declare that you are free and healed of all symptoms, sickness, and disease that is attacking your body. I know sickness can be a very scary place to be, but never give up hope. Some days will be harder than some, but continue to trust God.

Focus on God and His promises instead of what is happening in your body. We may experience pain that feels endless, circumstances that appear hopeless, or waiting that seems unbreakable. We may not experience healing the way we want it, but continue to trust God. Believe that He is always able and within reach.

Jesus reminds me that He is never out of my reach or without hope. He can do what no one else can do. Even though I didn't know what was happening in my body, I claimed my healing and continued to walk in it. To this day, those feelings still come back from time to time, but I have learned how to respond to them so they don't linger here anymore.

Chapter 3

~∾~

Process for Purpose: Yield, Trust, Wait and Pursue Purpose

Renew Your Mind: Change Your Perspective

Romans 12:2 - Do not conform to the pattern of this world, but be transformed by the renewing of your mind. Then you will be able to test and approve what God's will is—his good, pleasing and perfect will. (NIV).

According to this scripture, you can transform your way of thinking. I had to renew my mind in order to yield to my purpose. Have you ever heard the saying, "Where the mind goes, the man follows"? The enemy will work overtime for us to doubt God's Word and feel like giving up. Our minds can become bombarded with negative thoughts, worry, fear, and anxiety. These thoughts can lead to feelings of loneliness, rejection, shame, and unworthiness, etc. Changing the way you think and react is a process. It requires that you be intentional in doing so every day of your life.

When you learn the truth of God's Word and speak them, something will begin to transform in you. The truth of God's Word is like freedom from what was holding us captive for years. The lies and negative influences start to fall away, and the power of God's Word will begin to rise up in you. The mind can easily be persuaded to think negatively if we don't practice to take every thought captive to come in alignment with the Word of God. The enemy will whisper lies like "God doesn't care about what you're going through" or "Look how long you're going through that situation. Where is God?" Sometimes it is hard to take your thoughts captive when you are suffering for a long time; you tend to feel hopeless and pity yourself. There were times when I gave in to hopelessness and self-pity, but God would always send a word of encouragement my way; it could be a song, sermon or scripture. This would give me the strength to rise up and continue on my journey.

Stay in the Word of God so your mind can be renewed. As David said, *"Thy word is a lamp unto my feet and light unto my path." (Psalm 119:105).* That is what the Word of God is, if you meditate on it day and night. I found that meditating on scriptures each day helped me to shift my perspective of the situation and I started to look at it from a spiritual perspective rather than what I was seeing with my natural eyes. I found promises in the Bible that speak about my situation; I read them daily, wrote them on flash cards, and had them by my bedside. It gave me peace in knowing what the Word of God said about my situation.

Arm yourself with scripture each morning; memorise it and meditate on it throughout your day. Every time the devil comes at you with a negative thought, speak that scripture out loud or recite it in your mind. Once you have gotten a hold of its promises, it is hard for the enemy to fill your mind with lies and negativity. Freedom from negative thought patterns is not usually instant, but it comes by continually coming in agreement with the Word, thinking the Word, speaking the Word, and praying the Word. As we do these things, our mindset will begin to change; our minds and souls are healed, and we start to see our true identity in Christ through His Word. We will begin to establish our freedom.

Yield to the Process

LET GO AND LET GOD: SURRENDER TO HIS PLAN

What area of your life have you not surrendered to God? I learned that I must submit every area and aspect of my life to God in the process. You must yield to the process. Yield means to surrender. Yielding to the Holy Spirit means to surrender completely to the Spirit of God, giving Him total control of every area of your life. Surrender is telling God that we are not big enough to deal with all our worries and problems, and He must take over.

Yielding is a daily choice. When yielding is done through sincere and humble prayer, and we are able to honestly say, "Thy will be done," then we will see God's infinite good in our lives. Therefore, having a humble and submissive heart is a choice we make. Surrendering to God is not the easiest thing to do because our natural instincts urge us to move on with our plan on our timetable. It is especially hard when you are in the midst of a situation where you need an immediate answer. Yes, I know this is not easy to do, especially when you are used to being in control and doing things your way. Jesus said in order to be His disciple, you have to deny yourself, take up your cross daily and follow Him (see Matthew 16:24). Nobody likes pain, but going through these situations strengthens our faith muscles and causes us to grow spiritually. Sometimes without this pain, we are not able to grow to the next level where God wants us to be. For me personally, it was going through years of processing that caused me to get more intimate with God. It didn't just happen overnight; it took great work, intentionality and faith because there were days when I did not feel like yielding and just wanted to do things in my own flesh. That is one of the reasons the Bible tells us to walk in the Spirit so we don't fulfil the lust of the flesh (see Galatians 5:16). The flesh always wants what it thinks is best for you and not what God thinks.

When I remember why I am yielding every day, it gives me the strength to push even more. I think of the people who are out there waiting for my ministry to turn their lives around, and the generational curses that need to be broken so they are not passed down to my children or the next generation to come. Always have a why, and whenever you feel like you are going off course, just remind yourself about that why.

40

Maybe your why is to be the one to pull your family out of the generational curse and turn things around for your family.

Be intentional and give God your fresh surrender and "yes" each day. Be consistent, even if you have messed up some of the days. Don't stop yielding. It is in your time of yielding that God brings to the surface what is inside you that is hidden and will not surface unless you are pushed under the pressure that you are under. Sometimes, without pressure, we are not able to see what we are made up of.

It took some time for me to yield to the Lord. I was more concerned with what was happening to me and how I was going to fix my situation. I kept asking God why He allowed me to go through such public disgrace when He knew I was innocent. *Why didn't He just allow the person or persons to confess to what they had done so I was able to move on with my life?* That didn't happen in the time I was expecting. It was painful to put my reputation on the line, and it was a public disgrace. *"How was I going to bounce back from this?"* I wondered.

God is a good Father, and He wouldn't have allowed the situation to happen if He hadn't already placed the strength within you to handle what would come your way.

I spent the first year of my trial fighting in my own strength, which caused me to become miserable and fearful. Thoughts of the unknown kept running through my mind. I felt hopeless, as if God had let me down. Maybe you can relate to how I was feeling. It was definitely not a place to be, especially as a Christian. It would continue for days, weeks, and months. Whenever I had a court appearance, and it didn't go according to how I wanted it to go, I felt disappointed and discouraged all over again. *Where is God in all this? Doesn't He see me hurting and suffering? He knows I am innocent! Why won't He step in to help me?*

I sat in my pity party until I decided to pick myself up. I tried to throw in the towel many times, but God wouldn't let me. I honestly didn't realize that I was being processed for purpose. I thought I had done something wrong, and God was paying me back for all the sins I had committed before turning my life over to Him. I was a backslider and had just recommitted my life back to the Lord before I was arrested. I kept going to church Sunday after Sunday, and He would speak a word of encouragement to me through the pastor, but whenever I went to court, it would always be the opposite of the message I heard. It felt like the messages were cliché, and they left me feeling even more discouraged.

That episode of my life continued until I had an encounter with God. Yes, I was going to church, but I didn't have a personal relationship with God. I was living off the message preached by the pastor. I would jump, clap, and sing, but still felt empty. I always go back to thinking about my future and what was in store for me.

I had just finished my BBA at University and acquired a house for my sister and me. My sister's work contract was up at the time, and it wasn't renewed. She was attending Teachers College. I was the one taking care of the bills. I thought, "Lord, what else can go wrong now?" I lost my mom to cancer in 2005, and that was the biggest hit for me in my life. She was my mentor and motivator. I couldn't see myself living without her at that age. I didn't realize that God had started processing me from that time for the purpose He had for me.

Many of the great characters in the Bible had to go through their processing to be the great men and women God called them to be. It is a process. We must first be delivered from the things that would hinder us from walking in our purpose. I was reading my Bible, fasting, praying, and serving in church, but I did it all as a routine. My whole heart was not fully into it. In essence, I was a surface Christian doing things out of routine. Surface Christianity will not give you the power to cast out demons and command healing to be manifested; you must go deeper in God. You have to make His presence your dwelling place daily. The supernatural comes by going deep into the presence of God; by having intimacy with Him.

No one is immune to pain or suffering in this world, and there is no problem-free life. Life is a series of ups and downs. Jesus warned us that in this world, we would have problems (see John 16:33). God uses problems to draw us closer to Him. He also uses them to develop that Christ-like character in us, if we let Him. My most intimate worship comes from my place of brokenness. It is in our brokenness that we lose our pride. We have no other option but to rely on Jesus to fix the situation; only He can make it possible in the face of impossibility.

Sometimes we think we are perfect in our own eyes, but when pressure is applied, then we realize that pruning was necessary. Allow God to do His pruning in you; you will thank Him for it. In this imperfect world, we often see perfection by the way we attire ourselves or by our body image, but we forget to take a close look at the heart, which is the most important of them all. Men see the outward appearance, but God looks at the heart (see 1 Samuel 16:7).

The heart is very wicked and can easily become bitter, especially if we hold a lot of offenses on the inside. It can stay there and begin to fester, and that is where unforgiveness steps in; anger and hatred step in. Sometimes we say that we forgive someone, but most of the time, it is from the lips and not the heart. The Bible says that if we regard iniquity in our hearts, the Lord will not answer our prayers (see Psalm 66:18). Some of our unanswered prayers have to do with the state of our hearts.

God loves us and wants to answer our prayers. He doesn't want to withhold any good thing from us. Just yield to Him and allow Him to do great things through you. There are many things on this earth to be accomplished. God is looking for persons who are willing to be processed and to be used by Him to accomplish them. He needs a body to fill with the Holy Spirit to do signs and wonders.

The process can be painful and hard, but in the end, it will all be worth it when you see how many lives you have impacted because you endured the process. It is similar to being pregnant for nine months, and then it is time to give birth to that baby. The labour process is very hard and painful, but after seeing your beautiful baby, you forget the pain you just went through because of the joy and excitement over the baby. I encourage you to look at your processing in that way.

I have learned to grow through what I go through. I always try to make every experience a learning experience. *What lesson did I get from that, and how can I grow from the situation? What can I do better next time to alleviate this burden?* Don't hold back a certain area of your life from God thinking that He is not interested in it. He is interested in every area and aspect of your life; surrender it all to Him. He can handle your pain.

Don't look at the process as if God is punishing you for something you have done. If you look at it that way, you will become frustrated and feel like giving up. See your process as God perfecting you to do great work through you for the advancement of His kingdom.

Surrender Daily to the Process

Start each day by giving control to God. We have circumstances that can cause us to worry, fear, and become anxious each day. Surrendering to Jesus allows us to release our heavy burdens to Him and allows Him to take care of them. He loves us and cares about the things that overwhelmed us. Surrendering control to God is a daily, moment-by-moment choice. Surrender is hard when it is not done daily. Start each day with a prayer, inviting the Holy Spirit to fill you up.

We should pray every day for a fresh refilling of the Holy Spirit. Speak to God and acknowledge Him. Ask Him for guidance and direction for the day ahead. The enemy's plan is to cloud our minds with worry, doubts, and fears. The devil's desire is for there to be no room left for God in our lives. Surrendering to God becomes a lifestyle of daily giving it all to Him.

Whenever negative thoughts seek to invade our space, we must cut them off and give them to God immediately. God's mercies are new every morning, so what happened yesterday, last year, or a decade ago is completely gone. Carrying the past around will only take up space that should be occupied by God's goodness, grace, and favor. Renewing our minds in Christ means letting go of all the burdens He died to take from us.

Control is the hardest thing to give up because, without it, we feel vulnerable. We do not need to worry. God is already in control. We need to recognize His authority, move over, and let Him lead. He is the Creator of the Universe, so we can trust Him with each day. Letting go is scary at first, but the freedom in our minds and hearts will be worth it.

Surrender Your Plans to His Plan

God's plan and perspective is far greater than the plans we can imagine or have for our lives. Surrendering to God's plan means letting go of the plan we have for our lives. He knows more than we do and has every detail of our lives under control. When we surrender to His will, it gives us peace that settles our hearts and gives our minds rest. Our plans may seem like the best in our eyes, but in the eyes of God, it is nothing compared to all that He has in store for us. If we don't surrender to His plan, then we won't be able to walk in His best for our lives. Learn to surrender to His plans, even if it hurts. He knows what is best for us.

Chapter 4

Trust the Process

Proverbs 3:5-6 - Trust in the Lord with all thine heart; and lean not unto thine own understanding. In all thy ways acknowledge him, and he shall direct thy paths. (KJV).

How can you learn to trust the process? Do you struggle to trust God completely? Trusting God is trusting the process. When we learn to trust God's plan for our lives, we then begin to build trust in hard circumstances, knowing that, no matter what, He will come through for us. In any loving relationship, you must learn to trust. That is how it is with God; we must learn how to trust Him with every area and aspect of our lives because He is trustworthy.

I know it is hard to trust people at times, especially when you have been hurt many times in your life. But God commanded us in His Word to trust Him instead of putting our trust in things and people that can easily fail us. Trusting

49

God is the most important thing you can do when you don't know what to do or you don't have all the answers. Trust God, even when you don't understand. He opens doors, and He closes doors.

Hebrews 11:6 - And without faith it is impossible to please God, because anyone who comes to him must believe that he exists and that he rewards those who earnestly seek him. (NIV).

It Takes Faith to Trust God

Trust requires faith. Having faith is having trust. Trusting means choosing our faith over fear. As believers, we are called to walk by faith and not by sight. Faith allows us to see beyond and continue to keep our eyes on the prize. Faith gives us hope and confidence that everything will turn out good. Build your faith and grow through your process.

Faith keeps you going until you see the promises of God fulfilled in your life. Trust with your entire being, knowing that God has your back, and He will take care of you. He knows what is best, but to truly embrace what He has planned for you, you must fully trust Him. Let your faith be strengthened today, knowing that God is preparing you for what He wants to do through you. He is teaching you to trust Him and to grow in your faith and character. He grows our faith and ability to do what He has called us to do. God takes us through a process; will you trust the process? Trust Him knowing that the process will bring forth the promise.

It is so easy to lose faith when we are waiting for a long time. Our Christianity is centered around faith. Faith is the currency of heaven, and without it, you cannot please God. God wants us to grow in our faith as a child of God. That is why He tests us in the area of our faith. Are we going to believe Him or believe what the doctor or circumstances say? I have always found myself saying, "Lord, give me faith like Job." I didn't know what it meant until I had to face my own storms in life that required me to have faith like Job.

Now faith is the substance of things hoped for, the evidence of things not seen. (Hebrews 11:1 – NKJV).

If you get something right away that you pray for and you don't have to wait for it, that is not growing your faith. Faith requires us to grow in our walk with God. The more we believe, rely on, and trust God, the more our faith will grow. Just like Abraham, he had to believe God that the promise in his life will come to pass despite the many years he had to wait. Are we going to allow fear to cause us to forget the promises of God because what we are hoping for is taking a long time to manifest?

I know it is easier said than done. There are times when I waver in my faith because of how long the court matter lingered on, but I had to learn to have faith in the promise of God that it would work out for my good. It doesn't matter how long it takes, God's plan for my life is for good and not to cause me harm. I have learned to lift my faith despite the situation. I have seen God come through for me during those times when I lifted my faith regarding a matter. James 1:6-8 says, **"But let him ask in faith, with no doubting, for he who doubts is like a wave of the sea driven and tossed by the wind. For let not that man suppose that he will receive anything from the Lord; he is a double-minded man, unstable in all his ways." (NKJV).** We will not receive anything from our heavenly Father if we are wavering in our faith.

It is so easy for us to believe scientists and what the doctor says more than God. It would seem like non-Christians have more faith than Christians because of the risk they are willing to take. Faith is a risk; it is believing for something you haven't seen come to pass yet, hoping for it to happen. I know God is teaching me to grow my faith for where He is about to take me.

As I go through my season like Job, I have no doubt that the situation will work for my good. God will repay me double for my trouble just like Job. The Bible said that if we have faith as small as a mustard seed, we can move mountains (see Matthew 17:20). A mustard seed is very small in size but can bring forth a big, strong tree. Start somewhere and watch how big your faith can grow to believe in God for the impossible. There are times when we are waiting on God to do something, but God is really the one waiting on us. Faith is now; stay in the now. Your faith is going to turn things around. Live with the anticipation that it could happen today. Faith is what keeps us going until we see God do what He has promised. Faith causes us to say, "I may not see it yet, but if God promised it, I'm sure I will!" Remember, He is the God of the impossible, and all it takes is our faith to please Him.

Trust God's Promises, Not Your Fear

Psalm 56:3 - Whenever I am afraid, I will trust in You. (NKJV).

Fear is a part of being human, which is why it is emphasized so many times in the Bible. It is easy for us to panic and become anxious when the simplest of things in our lives go wrong. We fear countless things. I realize that when I am afraid, I am not trusting that God can handle my situation. Trusting God means choosing to believe His promises instead of our fears. We learn to be steadfast and secure when we fix our hearts on His promises. Many times we hold on to things that we cannot change. We internalize them and allow them to cause us to become depressed and anxious. Trust God enough to give it to Him. He will handle it. Dig into scriptures, study, memorize, meditate, and apply. Get familiar with the promises of God and stand on them. God never fails. If someone lets you down, God will never let you down. Trust in Him and His promises.

Trusting God Means Having a Personal Relationship With Him

We were created to have a personal relationship with God. An authentic relationship doesn't happen overnight. It is a process that takes time to grow and develop. In any relationship, you must be intentional about developing it every day. You can be going to church for years and don't have a personal relationship with God—knowing Him on an intimate level. When you are intimate with Him, you can differentiate His voice from the voice of the enemy. We need to include God in our daily lives. That means finding ways to connect and listen to Him every day. Start by fellowshipping with Him in prayer, spending time in His presence, reading His Word, praise and worship, love and trusting in Him daily. Every minute, throughout the course of your day, meditate on His Word. Having a personal relationship with God is the best life decision you will ever make.

Trust God, Not Your Emotions or Feelings

Psalm 42:5 - Why are you cast down, O my soul? And why are you disquieted within me? Hope in God, for I shall yet praise Him for the help of His countenance. (NKJV).

Emotions are fickle—they change frequently and often without notice. Today you are up and down tomorrow. We cannot just rely on feelings to take us through our time of processing. Don't let your emotions call the shots.

There are days when I feel like I am drowning in my situation, and the next day I feel as if I could conquer the world. I have learned that my emotions can go up and down, but God is dependable. His feelings towards me or the situation that I am going through never change. He is still there working on my behalf, despite my wanting to throw in the towel. It is easy to make decisions based on what we think, feel, and want, but we must be very careful not to be led by our emotions. Emotions are given to us by God; that is part of being human.

Emotions are an important part of enjoying life; it doesn't mean all our emotions are bad. We shouldn't allow our feelings to control us. We can learn, enjoy, or be guided by our feelings. We should let our feelings be guided by the Word of God. This will help us to better manage our emotions instead of allowing them to manage us. Trusting God is more than a feeling; it is a choice to have faith in what He says, even when your feelings or situation would have you believe something different. Trusting God is not about ignoring your feelings or reality. It is not about pretending that everything is okay when it isn't. Trusting God is believing and being obedient, even when things are difficult in your life.

Trust God's Will Over Your Own Way

Proverbs 16:3 - Commit your works to the Lord, and your thoughts will be established. (NKJV).

What happens when you don't get the results you are looking for? It is hard to trust the will of God sometimes, especially when it is not in accordance with the plans we have for our lives. I knew God wanted good for me, but I honestly thought my plans were better. When I prayed, my prayers would be mostly petitions, asking God to bless the plans I had for my life rather than asking Him what He had planned for me. Walking in your own will can be frustrating and cause you to feel burnt out. I had to recommit the works of my hands and the desires of my heart to God. I sought His wisdom and surrendered my plans to Him with trust, knowing that He could bring them to pass. God has better things ahead for us, and His will for our lives will always be best. When we seek God in all things, we realize that our heart's true desire can only be found in Him. *Lord, help us to trust You, surrender and follow Your lead.*

Trust in His Strength, Not Yours

2 Corinthians 12:9 - And he said unto me, My grace is sufficient for thee: for my strength is made perfect in weakness. Most gladly therefore will I rather glory in my infirmities, that the power of Christ may rest upon me. (KJV).

We have moments of human frailty and weakness, but it is in those moments when we are at our weakest and vulnerable point that we can draw on God's strength. We are not called to rely on our own strength. There will be days when you feel as if you cannot go on, and that is when you need to lean into God for strength.

There are days when your challenge seems impossible. Of course, it is impossible when we try to do it in our own strength, but God's strength working through our faith will turn the impossible into possible. It is easy to get burnt out when we operate in our own strength. Our human strength is limited, but God's power is limitless. God's strength is a shield from feelings of anxiety, panic, and depression. When we fully put our trust in Him, He walks alongside us. God's power within us will enable us to stand strong to walk through our situations. When you give Him your trust, He will fill you with power.

Trust His Timing

God's timing is always perfect, but we can get frustrated because our human nature wants immediate results. I have learned to trust God's timing in my night seasons. I know it is easier said than done. I have been there, and I am still learning. Trust requires us to place our timing in God's hand, believing that His timing in our lives is always perfect. God is never late, never early, but always on time. God's timing always feels like a long delay. However, I have learned that

God's timing allows us to grow spiritually in our faith and character.

God's Word has never failed, and it never will. In order to cooperate with God's timing, we must let Him make the relevant changes in our lives. God's delay was used to re-teach me about trust because I was lacking it in that season of my life. You can trust His timing because if He gives a promise, it will be fulfilled. God makes everything beautiful in His perfect timing; trust it.

Trust in His Unfailing Love

Psalm 32:10 - Many sorrows shall be to the wicked: but he that trusteth in the Lord, mercy shall compass him about. (KJV).

There are times we may feel lonely or unworthy of love. God's love is always greater than the love that anyone on this earth can give us. He loves us so much that He died on the cross for us; His love is eternal. No matter what, God will always love us. No matter how many times we have messed up, His love never changes. God's love is unconditional. Nothing can separate us from the love of God (see Romans 8:39). When you are confident of God's love for you, you know that no matter what you face, He is with you. God's love will last forever; trust in it.

I didn't just develop trust in God's love overnight; it was a struggle for me, but I had to make up my mind, with His help, that I was going to trust Him through my process and allow Him to bring forth His promise in me. Initially, I thought, if God really loved me, then why was I going through all those hardships? But thank God for His Holy Spirit who has been with me all the way. He has allowed me to experience God's love on a daily basis. I chose not to become bitter, but better, and that was when I started to see my faith strengthening. Your trust is not foolish because our God is good and faithful.

Trust that all things will work together for your good.

Romans 8:28 - And we know that in all things God works for the good of those who love him, who have been called according to his purpose. (NIV).

I use the story of Job and Joseph to bring me hope.

There was a man in the land of Uz, whose name was Job; and that man was blameless and upright, and one who feared God and shunned evil. (Job 1:1 - NKJV).

Job went through a great ordeal of suffering. He lost his possessions and children, and his health was attacked as well. So, why do the righteous suffer? Job was blameless and had to go through all of that, so none of us is exempt from suffering because we are living in a fallen world. Job's attitude towards suffering was admirable. Despite what he was going through, he refused to curse God, even when his wife was telling him to do so. *"My God,"* I thought to myself, *"Some of us would have cursed God and given up if we were in Job's position."* Job questions God in anger without giving up. Job passed his test, and so can you.

It is not easy when those who should be there for you are the ones talking against you, especially when you are going through a great ordeal of suffering. Job's friends saw his suffering as him sinning against God, and now God was punishing him for all the wrongs he had done. They believed that suffering had to do with retribution. In all that he was going through, Job learned that God is sovereign, free to do as He chooses, and is not obligated to answer us (see Job 23). In the end, after Job prayed for his friends, he was restored double for his trouble. Hallelujah! This taught me not to hold unforgiveness in my heart against those who have done me wrong.

I saw my experience as a Job experience. I didn't lose all that Job lost, but my job, finances, health, child, and husband were affected by all this. We can't endure in our own strength. We must lean into God for endurance to go through the ups and downs of life. You must build, and continue relying on God to build, your endurance because life happens to the best of us, often without any warning. The God of endurance will give you the strength to run the race and finish well. Look to Him.

Joseph was thrown into a pit by his brothers, sold as a slave to Potiphar, and was appointed head of Potiphar's estate until Potiphar's wife started to develop a sexual interest in

Joseph. He was not interested in her like that and kept on refusing until one day she forced herself on him. He refused again, and she told her husband lies that Joseph was trying to be intimate with her. Joseph was then placed in prison, where he was favoured and promoted. While in prison, Joseph met two of Pharaoh's officials who were incarcerated: the chief cupbearer and the chief baker. Joseph successfully interpreted their dreams. The cupbearer was released from prison and remembered Joseph two years later when Pharaoh had a dream, and none of his advisors could interpret it. They sent for Joseph, and he interpreted Pharaoh's dream correctly and was appointed second to Pharaoh. There arose a great famine in Egypt and Canaan, as interpreted by Joseph from Pharaoh's dreams. Joseph's brothers who were living in Canaan had to go to Egypt to seek food in that same country where Joseph was the ruler. They visited twice for food, and on the second visit, Joseph revealed himself to them (see Genesis 45:1).

We could see here that what the enemy meant for evil, God turned it around for Joseph's good (see Genesis 50:20). Joseph's story brings out the proper attitude towards difficulty and being mistreated. He could have used his power against his brothers for evil, but he didn't. He showed them kindness instead. That is another lesson on forgiveness. I don't know who was responsible for getting me arrested for fraudulent cheques passed on to me in the line of duty, but I chose to forgive whomever it might be. The delay and setback in the case was a blessing in disguise for me. I was able to plan my wedding all by myself and help my previous church sister to plan hers. I was able to stay with my daughter from birth until she was grown, and I was able to spend quality time each day with God in prayer, worship and the reading of His Word. I was able to get mentorships and be a part of seminars. I was able to go on the path of discovering my purpose. I had my freedom. I was able to move in my own time. That season of my life, even though I wouldn't wish what happened to me on my worst enemy, has taught me a lot about God, myself, and life. It taught me patience, perseverance, endurance, forgiveness, humility, and how to build my faith. The Holy Spirit has really taught me a lot, and I am able to share my experience in this book with others. This book was given to me by God after coming out of a seminar. The Spirit of God said to me, "Write" and I started writing, and it felt as if I couldn't stop. I was amazed at how much I had written that day in such a short time.

God has divinely allowed every season of our lives in His sovereign wisdom. Those seasons may include some type of hardship, just like Joseph and Job. God truly gave me the revelation of Romans 8:28 - **And we know that in all things God works for the good of those who love him, who have been called according to his purpose. (NIV).**

On the first day of my arrest, when all those unanswered questions were running through my mind, all I could hear was this scripture. I didn't understand what it meant at first until God began to open my understanding to the revelation that it doesn't matter how bad my situation looked, it will work out for my good because I am called by Him for purpose. Even though, on some days, it doesn't seem like it because of the constant delaying of the court case, I kept asking God, "When will it work out for my good?" All I heard was, "Just trust Me." Because I know that all things will work out for my good, I left it in the hands of God and shifted my focus from the crisis to Christ, and that was when I started to see God working in my life. I started to feel that peace that He promised us that passeth all understanding. My joy went to another level, and that was when I decided to live my life totally yielded to Him.

I told God to use my situation for His glory despite how painful and how long it is taking. I made up my mind to yield to the process and allow God to do His great work in and through me. I was tired of fighting in my own strength; it caused me to feel weary, discouraged, and disappointed.

Everything you have been through was necessary for where God is taking you. Just because bad things happen doesn't mean you are out of the will of God.

Chapter 5

Waiting In The Process

Isaiah 40:31 - But they that wait upon the Lord shall renew their strength; they shall mount up with wings as eagles; they shall run, and not be weary; and they shall walk, and not faint. (KJV).

Waiting on God is a process. Many people want change, but they don't want to go through their season of waiting. The process purifies our intentions as we learn to seek God and not just what He has to offer. God has placed a seed inside us, and for that seed to grow, it needs to be nurtured. No one plants a seed today and expects it to grow the next day. It takes time for that seed to grow in order to reap a harvest. As it is in the natural, so it is in the spiritual. It takes time for our seed to grow.

We must be willing to wait long enough for our spiritual seeds to produce the harvest for the glory of God. Waiting serves an important purpose in the process. No one said that waiting is easy. We live in a fast-paced world where most things are instant, for example, the microwave, washing machine, fast food, and get-rich-quick schemes. God's kingdom doesn't operate like this; it takes time for growth and character development. In the meantime, as Paul states, **"Let us not become weary in doing good..." (Galatians 6:9 - NIV).** Don't give in to that spirit of weariness; that is what the enemy wants. Your breakthrough might just be one prayer, fast, or worship away. Even if you give in today, get back up tomorrow and continue your journey. Don't live there.

Waiting can be hard at times, but when you keep your eyes on the promises of God, it gives you the strength to go forth each day to patiently wait on God. The more patient you are, the more able you are to deal with situations that would easily overwhelm others.

You can still be fruitful in your season of waiting, as long as you are connected to the vine and make Him your confidence and hope by trusting in Him. Don't be passive or a complainer while in your season of waiting. We are still learning as we go through the process.

Sometimes it is hard to see the reason for waiting. There are things I am still waiting on, and I wish they would work out immediately, but I am still waiting. There is so much God wants to do through us in our waiting season.

Pray Without Ceasing While You Wait

1 Thessalonians 5:17 - Pray without ceasing. (KJV).

While you are waiting for God's promises to fulfil in your life, pray without ceasing. Waiting for the promises of God means constantly interceding and aligning our thoughts and heart in preparation for the promises. God wants us to come boldly to His throne. *Without ceasing* does not mean praying for 24 hours, seven days a week, and never getting off our knees. It means that all throughout the day, we should maintain a prayerful attitude. Praying without ceasing means talking to God while driving, washing, shopping, working, or performing any other everyday tasks. Everything you do can be spending time with God; just invite Him to be a part of it. He loves it when we communicate with Him. Our prayer and the time we spend talking to God acts as nourishment to our soul. Pray continually and pray constantly.

"Prayer is an earthly license for heavenly interference."
—*Myles Munroe.*

Don't let the fire on your altar run out. A powerful Christian is a praying Christian. The Bible commands us to pray without ceasing; it doesn't matter how you feel. There is power in prayer. Prayer will release the power of God on our behalf. Jesus spent hours praying to His Father because He knows how powerful prayer is. Prayer is an important part of our spiritual defense.

Praying without ceasing doesn't necessarily mean to stop and go to your prayer closet every minute to pray. It means you can make prayer a part of everything you are doing. You can pray softly while in the office at your desk, doing your work. You can pray under your breath while shopping, showering, washing the dishes, doing laundry, on the bus, or in a taxi.

Cry if you must while praying, but don't cease to pray. Push past your emotions. The flesh doesn't want us to pray, so it will always put up a resistance. You must be disciplined and intentional about it. I had stopped praying about my situation for a long time because each time I prayed, nothing seemed to be changing. I would pray about everything except my court case.

One day, while fasting, I said to God, "Why am I not getting an answer to what I'm going through?" The Holy Spirit said to me, "Because you have stopped praying about it a long time ago." He pointed me to Luke 18 with the unjust judge and the widow. The widow was constantly going to the judge asking him to avenge her, and he wouldn't. When he got so annoyed with her constantly coming to him, he avenged her of her adversary. That was a "Wow" moment for me. I got the revelation.

God was telling me to pray without ceasing, whether I got the answer right away or not. I should never cease to pray. It can really be frustrating when you are praying and nothing is happening. It is discouraging and disappointing. I have been there. Let me encourage you as I continue to encourage myself: don't cease to pray. I made a commitment to continue to pray about my case until I see the manifestation come to pass. I got another revelation: for me to get a breakthrough in the natural, I needed to pray for it to break in the spiritual.

In Daniel 10:12-14, from the first day Daniel prayed, his prayer was heard by God and a release was sent out, but it was held up in the realm of the spirit for twenty-one days by the Prince of Persia. The angel, Michael, had to come and release it. Daniel was unaware of what was happening until it was revealed to him by the messenger from God in a vision. Most times, the answers to our prayers are released in the spiritual, but there are forces fighting against the answers reaching us. The enemy wants us to believe that God doesn't answer our prayers. Daniel didn't give up on seeking God. He held on until there was a manifestation to his prayer. It is possible for us to prevail in prayer if we do not give up on continual prayer and fasting.

In 1 Kings 18:41-43, Eljah prayed seven times before the rain came. He could have given up after the first or second attempt, but he held on to his faith, believing that God would send the rain, and He did the seventh time. What if Elijah had given up? There would not have been an abundance of rain. I don't know what you are going through or how long you are going through it, but be encouraged to not give up. I am also encouraging myself. Your abundance is coming, so continue praying, trusting, and believing in God. It doesn't matter how long it takes, continue to contend for the manifestation of your prayer and prophecy. Remember, life is spiritual, and there are many forces fighting against us that want to keep us stuck in generational curses and bondages. These forces fight against our breakthrough and try to keep us stagnant.

I was living a prayerless life for a while. I was praying a 5-10 minute prayer in the mornings before work and before going to bed at night. I wasn't really spending any quality time in prayer with God. I always tell myself that I cannot pray long or I don't know what to say. Thank God that has changed. I am now praying without ceasing. Thanks to my praying church WAFIF, every morning at 4:30 in the morning, we meet for an hour to pray. During the course of the day, I would spend an hour of quiet time with God, and I would incorporate prayer in my activities throughout the day. Prayer has become a part of me.

I went on a journey to develop my prayer life. I bought books about prayer. I learned a lot about prayer. I didn't know how important it was to really pray until something happened. God gave us prayer as a weapon against the enemy, and the enemy knows how effective our prayer is, so he will put all kinds of distractions in our way just to keep us from praying. When we pray and truly pray, then God will act on our behalf. The answers might not come right away, but He will send the answers right on time. God doesn't operate illegally. He wants us to give Him the legal right to act. James 5:16 says the effectual fervent prayer of a righteous man availeth much. Don't just pray, but pray fervently and according to the will of God.

Spend Quiet Time in Solitude With God

Psalm 16:11 - Thou wilt shew me the path of life: in thy presence is fulness of joy; at thy right hand there are pleasures for evermore. (KJV).

Quiet time is a personal time you spend with God alone reading and meditating on scriptures and journaling what He lays on your heart. Having a quiet mind causes your relationship with God to go to another level because you can sense the presence of God strongly and are more aware of the impressions He is laying on your heart. It is very important for us to spend quality time alone with God.

When I am still before the Lord, I can hear His voice more clearly. I remember in 2017, months after I was arrested, I was sitting in silence in the presence of God when the Holy Spirit impressed on my heart to reach out to a particular friend. I sent a text to the person, who replied and said, "So strange though, can you believe it? Just this evening, just before you texted me, I was in my car thinking about how you are managing and that I would give you some money to offset things.The person also went on to say: It is very strange that you would say the very same thing." Wow. This is amazing.. True testimony, the thought came so clear to me out of the blue."

My place of employment hadn't started paying me my quarterly salary yet, and I had just purchased my house so I had a mortgage to pay. My bank account was so low at the time because I used up most of my savings to pay the opening and closing deposit for the house. I was worried and panicking while God was taking care of my needs behind the scenes.

I find that whenever I don't spend time in the presence of God, I tend to feel miserable and agitated compared to when I spend time in His presence. In His presence there is fullness of joy (see Psalm 16:11). Having a quiet time with God is not as complicated as we think; it is just being in the presence of God and allowing Him to speak to us. We can get so used to speaking and not listening to what the Spirit of God is saying to us about the problems we have just prayed to Him about.

It was in my quiet time that I received answers to problems that was baffling me for months. By sitting and listening to God in stillness, I received instructions to problems I was seeking a solution for. Quiet time is a skill that takes practice, discipline, intentionality, and consistency. You can start with five minutes each day, and by doing it consistently, you find that you grow, and your quiet time starts to expand more as you go along.

I implore you, spend quality time in the presence of God. He wants to speak to us and is longing for us, His children, to have that intimate relationship with Him.

Let me share this testimony with you. I applied for my daughter's visa, and we were waiting for the embassy to

72

email us to take in the documents. One Sunday night, in my quiet time, the Spirit of God said to me that my daughter's visa was granted. I wrote it down. Two days later, the embassy sent my husband an email requesting the documents. I was in awe. All I could say was "Thank You, Jesus." Within that same week, she got the ten-year visa. God is so amazing! When we spend time in His presence, we will realize how much He really speaks to us, but are we listening to what He is saying?

In 2021, I was facing unknown health challenges and was from doctor to doctor without any diagnosis, frustrated and googling every symptom I felt for an answer. After I had enough of the doctors, I was sitting on my veranda one day in silence when the Spirit of God said to me, "Just rest in Me." He gave me specific instructions on what to do. Thank God I was obedient to the voice of God. That was when I started to see things shift for the better in my health. Before then, I was too busy going about my business, trying to find answers without fully tuning in to the source who had the answer to what I was going through.

I would be in my quiet time, and the Holy Spirit would give me a word for persons. When I reached out to the person, it was exactly what they needed to hear or a confirmation of what God had laid on their heart. Quiet time with God is a very integral part of our life and relationship with God. Practice it every day; it is like medicine.

Worship While You Wait

Acts 16:25 - And at midnight Paul and Silas prayed, and sang praises unto God: and the prisoners heard them. (KJV).

According to the Merriam-Webster dictionary, worship is honouring or showing reverence to a divine being or supernatural power. Worship can be a key to waiting well. Your worship is a weapon that can be used to win battles. There is power when you worship God. Breakthrough happens when you worship God because it shuts out the enemy. Worship your way through your difficult seasons.

David was a worshipper. He worshipped God in the valley and on the mountaintop. This helped to restore David's soul; it helped him remember God's faithfulness and take his focus off the situations he was facing. Turn on some worship music, and it will turn your focus from your problems to the only One who is worthy of your praise and worship. Whenever I feel down in my spirit, I will turn on some worship music and locate myself in the presence of God. Try it; I guarantee that it is going to work.

Make the choice to be obedient to God and worship Him while you wait. Give Him true, undiluted worship, even in your brokenness. In the same way He sent an earthquake to shake the prison door open for Paul and Silas, He will do the same for you when you worship Him. Despite what you are going through, make worship a lifestyle.

Wait With Patience

Psalm 27:14 - Wait on the Lord: be of good courage, and he shall strengthen thine heart: wait, I say, on the Lord. (KJV).

What is your waiting posture? Are you waiting and complaining? Where you complain, you will remain. It is one thing to wait on God, but if you are not waiting in the right posture, you will miss out on what God has for you and wants to do through you. We can get impatient, especially when there is so much uncertainty. We like to have everything figured out. If we wait the wrong way, we will be miserable, but if we decide to wait God's way, we can become more patient and enjoy the wait. It takes a lot of practice, but as we let God help us in our situations, we develop patience. Patience is only developed through trials, so we must not run from difficult situations.

"But let patience have its perfect work, that you may be perfect and complete, lacking nothing."(James 1:4 – NKJV).

Patience is a virtue; it is a characteristic that develops our trust in God. To wait and be patient is to trust that God is working in your life, even when you can't see or understand what He is doing at the time. God reveals His character and love during our time of patience. While we wait, we need to lean on Him.

Patience begins by changing the way we view things. Our perspective tends to be dimmed when we are impatient. All we see is our self; needs, desires, and circumstances. We struggle to see from the perspective of God and how small our problems are in His sight. All we need to do is exercise patience and allow Him to work it out.

Patience is a fruit of the Spirit and an attribute of maturity as a Christian. Patience says, "I trust God. He's bigger than my problems, even though it hurts." I know it is hard to be patient when you are waiting for God to intervene in your health condition, financial struggles, problems on the job, and problems in the marriage. I have been there, and it is only by the grace of God that I was able to wait patiently for God to intervene in my situation. Be still and know that He is God (see Psalm 46:10). Allow patience to have its good work in you.

Prepare in Your Waiting Season

Should we just sit back and be passive? Is that what we should do? Or should we be doing something while waiting? *Preparing* is an active verb. Waiting is not supposed to be passive. Preparation is the key for where God wants to take you. Our waiting period is always a preparatory ground for the next level of our lives if we allow it. Prepare for what you have been praying for. Waiting can sometimes give us the feeling that we should sit back and do nothing, but that is not how it is in God's kingdom. I learned to be active in my season of waiting by working on the areas in my life that need to be developed and letting go of habits that aren't pleasing to God. As you wait on God to fulfil His promise to you, begin to prepare.

We need to wait until we give birth to the characteristics and qualities that are necessary and relevant for the next season of our lives. While you wait on what is next, what do you need to improve on in your life? What skills do you need to acquire for the next level? What wisdom and knowledge do you need that will prepare you for the next level? Is there a behaviour you can improve on? How about building a deeper relationship with God?

If you look at your waiting period as a season of punishment, you won't see the beauty in that season. It was in my season of waiting that I developed my prayer life, learned how to worship God in depth, learned more about His promises, and gained knowledge in areas I did not have knowledge of before. I attended mentorship sessions, read books, watched seminars, and served. My level of patience and endurance began to grow. I was able to build my faith and grow my strength. Whatever you are going through may be very painful and unbearable, but I want to encourage you: Don't waste your time while in the waiting season. Prepare. There is something within you that is about to be birthed. Give God something to work with, and He will show up.

Wait With Expectancy

Psalm 5:3 - My voice shalt thou hear in the morning. O Lord; in the morning will I direct my prayer unto thee, and will look up. (KJV).

Are you expecting your situation to turn around? Expectancy is the breeding ground for miracles. Expectancy is knowing that you are not waiting in vain and that any day could be the day of your breakthrough. There is an anticipation in your spirit. The situation may not look good, but when you are waiting with expectancy, you are not moved by what you see. Farmers wait confidently for their crops because they know their crops will come up. That is the way we are to wait on God's promises.

At one point, my heart got sick because I had stopped waiting with expectation because of how long the situation is taking to manifest. I had given up on the matter and just started living with an attitude of "Oh, well. If it happens, it happens." I felt like things were never going to change. God doesn't want us to wait that way. He wants us to wait, knowing that He will come through for us no matter how long it takes. We must learn to trust His timing. While we are expecting our healing to manifest, start believing it is already done and thank God in advance.

Serve While You Wait

Mark 10:43 - But so shall it not be among you: but whosoever will be great among you, shall be your minister. (KJV).

Serving in church or serving others can be a great way to take our eyes off our own troubles. Serving is helping others. I have learned that it is good to be a blessing to others while waiting on God for our promises and restoration to manifest in our lives. I encouraged and gave to others in my season of waiting. This experience taught me to focus on other's needs instead of my own. I too was being encouraged and refreshed. God will reward your sacrifice.

You don't need to have the gift of service to serve in the house of God or to serve others. Instead of waiting for your circumstances to change in order to serve, why don't you do it now. God forbid, things never change; are you going to just sit there in your sorry state when there are others out there waiting on what you have inside you? Are you waiting for your talents and giftings to manifest? I find that whenever I am serving or volunteering, I tend to focus less on what I am going through and more on how I can be of service to others. Don't serve half-heartedly, but do it wholeheartedly and watch God.

Don't wait until you get out of your circumstance to give God your all. Give Him everything while in the situation. Step out of your comfort zone and try something different—

something that challenges you or your routine even a little bit. Try something that stretches you, something that has the potential to make you better. Walk in your purpose. Let no one stand in your way. You were made for more.

Keep Your Eyes On The Big Picture While You Wait

What is your big picture? How do you see your story? My big picture is to see everyone I encounter become free and walk in the purpose that God has for their lives. So, whenever I feel overwhelmed and feel like throwing in the towel, I reflect on my big picture—my why. Why am I enduring this process? Why don't I give up and continue with life as usual? Having a big picture keeps me grounded and steadfast despite the difficulty of the situation. It pushes me to give you the motivation and drive to go on.

We must remind ourselves that it is not about us but about God and those who are waiting on us to pull them out of the darkest places in their lives into God's marvelous light. I encourage you, if you don't have a why or big picture, ask God to help or show you your big picture. While Jesus was on the cross, His big picture was Him dying to save us from a life of eternal sin, so He endured the cross, died, rose again, and is now with His Father in heavenly places.

What I learned about God is that He will never allow you hardship if He didn't want to bring out the best in you. He will never leave you empty-handed. I know it can be overwhelming, overbearing, frustrating and you may be at the end of the road. Just hold on a little while longer, and always keep your big picture at the forefront of your mind.

Find A Community And Align Yourself

Ecclesiastes 4:9-10 - Two are better than one; because they have a good reward for their labour. For if they fall, the one will lift up his fellow: but woe to him that is alone when he falleth; for he hath not another to help him up. (KJV).

Have you ever heard the saying, "Atmosphere is everything"? Pray and ask God to align you with the right people for you. Your destiny-helpers are people who will encourage you and speak into your life. They refuse to throw pity parties with you, but they see the best in you and will push you to greatness. It is very important to be careful of those who speak in your life, especially when you are going through the darkest season in your life.

In January 2022, I felt strongly in my spirit that the Lord was telling me to shift my atmosphere. I thought it was my atmosphere in regard to where I was living. Every message I heard from different preachers was saying, "Shift your atmosphere." My husband, daughter, and I left Kingston and went by my house in Old Harbour to spend some days hoping that there would be an improvement in how I was feeling each day. Nothing was changing, even though I shifted my atmosphere. I kept hearing the message and was still in dialogue with God about what I was sensing. It was not until I shifted my place of worship that I started seeing the hands of God moving in my life.

Sometimes we are stuck in a season of life and refuse to move because we are so comfortable there. You must know when your season has come to an end and move on. I was obedient to the Spirit of God and did exactly what I was sensing at the time. I left my previous church and went to another church where I started to see the hand of God moving in my life. I was strengthened spiritually to wage war against the enemy.

One Monday morning, while sitting on the veranda meditating, I heard the Holy Spirit say to me, "Rest in Me. I want to download something in your spirit." I realized that I was resting, but not in the Lord. I was resting in my own strength. That day, I felt a sense of peace come over me. He reminded me to cast my cares upon Him because He cares for me. All that time I thought I was resting in God, but I was just trying to get healed in my own strength. Jesus had already borne all my infirmities (see Matthew 8:17).

Job's friends and wife were not the best influence for him when he was facing his hardship. His wife told him to curse God and die, and his friends were being judgmental about his situation. In our place of darkness, we are going to come across friends or even family who will tell you to forget the whole Christian thing because it is not going anywhere or

God is not answering our prayers. That is the time you need to decide whose voice you listen to.

I am a self-motivated person at heart, but it was such a privilege to align myself with a church community that really helped me. There were many different programmes there to keep me focused and allow me to grow in all areas of my life. This atmosphere really helped me to grow, keep my eyes off what I was going through and focus more on God and my purpose. If you are truly connected and aligned with your church community, it really helps with going through your process, and your life will never be the same. As I heard the Spirit of God say, "Align to be realigned," I had to truly align myself in order to be realigned.

Get an accountability partner who will hold you accountable, help push you towards your purpose, and gently pick you up when you fall. If you are not a Christian or not a part of a church community, ensure you are connected to the right people. Victors are not those with a victim mentality. Victors are those who see the glass half-full rather than half-empty. They are the optimists, not the pessimists; the positive, not the negative; the faith-ers, not the doubters; the grateful, not the ungrateful. They speak into your spirit when you are going through your night seasons. Having the wrong person speaking in your ears will cause you to abort the purpose God has for your life. So, who is speaking in your ears, or who is advising you in life?

Wait With Intentionality

Intentionally means deliberately, on purpose. Wait on the Lord purposefully with a spirit of determination to seek Him daily; put Him at the center of your life. Keep your eyes on God and look to Him for direction. Stay in His presence, and He will show you the way.

Living intentionally may sound simple, but it is not easy. Life is filled with challenges, and we need to constantly renew our hearts and minds and be transformed to be like Christ.

The word *intentional* means to be deliberate or act on purpose. If we are not deliberate about waiting on God, we can be easily frustrated when things don't happen in our timing. I had to make up my mind that I was going to be intentional about waiting on God, even when my flesh didn't want to comply. It can be so draining sometimes, but what I realized is that when I set my mind on purpose, it pushes me beyond my feelings. Waiting can be hard, and that is why it needs to be intentional.

"Hope deferred maketh the heart sick: but when the desire cometh, it is a tree of life." (Proverbs 13:12 - KJV).

Did you know that your heart can become sick even as a Christian serving and waiting on God? Have you ever struggled because you know God can do anything, but you just can't understand why He is not intervening in your situation right now?

Yes, I have been there; my heart got sick at a point. With each passing year and no end to my impending court case in sight, I was trying to hang on to hope, but it got harder with each passing year. I started living life out of a routine without any form of enjoyment. I was merely existing and not living; the wait was too long and frustrating. It felt like I had no one standing up for me, not even God. On every occasion, before going to court, I would fast, pray, and ask for prayer. However, nothing seemed to be working. My heart was hurting because of the constant putting off of the court case with no apparent logical reasoning. What I learned though is that there are some seasons in life that you can't fast and pray away. If God allows it, then He will give you the grace and strength to get through it. If He doesn't solve it right away, He will sustain you through it until it comes to an end.

I got to a point where I stopped praying because it felt like my prayers were not working. When people who knew about the situation asked me about it, I would feel a bit agitated and want to change the subject. It was a disappointing kind of season that caused me to question my life and try to fix things myself. My way of fixing my situation was with my thoughts. I would think about the worst that could happen in the case and assume that that was the way God wanted my life to be. I didn't realize that those were lies that the enemy wanted me to think and dwell on. Satan likes to use our unmet expectations and disappointments to consume our hearts to make it even sicker while waiting on God.

One day, while in my quiet time with God, I asked Him, "Why is it that the court case is taking so long to come to an end?" He said to me, "Luke 18:1." When I turned to the scripture, it read, **"men ought always to pray, and not to faint;" (KJV).** He said, "You have stopped praying about it, so how can I intervene when you are not giving Me access to it?" I was in awe. I remember hearing a minister say that it has to first happen in the spiritual before it can be manifested in the natural. I repented that day and decided to spend at least an hour each day praying to God about it. I didn't just pray but prayed from the place of victory that it is already done.

God wants us to look to Him and pour out our hearts to Him. Tell Him how you feel because He already knows. It is pointless to pretend, as this only causes your heart to become sicker. Your life may be dark and confusing today, but there is power in your prayer. It may seem like there is nothing changing, but God is doing a great work behind the scenes. We don't always know when, where and how. We can only continue to pray without ceasing, trusting that God will turn our situation around for our good.

My situation has taught me to yield to the process, trust God, and wait while He processes me for my next level. It wasn't always easy, but it was worth it.

Delayed But Not Denied

If you are going through a long process, it doesn't mean God has forgotten you. I felt that way as months turned into years going to court without any end in sight to my court case. It made me think at one point that God had forgotten about me.

Purpose is a lonely road and, at some point, you are going to feel forgotten and alone when others who were there for you at first are no longer by your side. What I have learned is that people are there for a season, and once their season in your life comes to an end, they will no longer be running with you in the next season. Where God wants to take you requires a different you and a different set of people. Those people are called your destiny helpers. They will run with you until the fulfilment of purpose, and even after. They are there for a lifetime.

Let me encourage you—as I encourage myself—to hang in there just a little while longer. It doesn't matter how long it takes, God will come through for you in His way and in His own timing.

Sometimes we miss what God wants to do in our lives because we are looking for Him to do it a particular way. Don't miss your season of blessings because you are expecting Him to move a particular way or use a particular person. Even though it is taking so long for the breakthrough to come to pass, it doesn't mean you will never get to where God wants to take you. You will walk in everything God promised you. God is not limited by time or seasons; He is the Creator of it all.

I sometimes feel like I am waiting around for no reason, but while I may have been delayed, I have not been denied. Hold on, even if it is just by a thread; your process is purposeful. It will train, discipline, and prepare you for your promised land.

Think about the story of David and Goliath. David killed a lion and a bear who were trying to attack his sheep. That may have seemed insignificant to David and others at the time, but God was preparing David for something bigger to come. Goliath was so big that the army of God didn't wanted to face him. But David, by the strength and grace of God, was able to take Goliath down because of the experience he had with the lion and bear. Hold on, just like David; your Goliath will come to an end one day.

Ask God to help you submit to the process of delay and to give you strength, grace, and endurance while you wait patiently for His plans to be fulfilled in your life. Ask Him to help you remain focused so you do not easily become distracted. Weeping may endure for a night, but joy comes in the morning (see Psalm 30:5). Your breakthrough is on its way! Don't give up!

Chapter 6

Don't Waste Your Pain: Pursue Purpose

Jeremiah 29:11 - For I know the thoughts that I think toward you, saith the Lord, thoughts of peace, and not of evil, to give you an expected end. (KJV).

Have you ever found yourself asking, "What is my purpose? What am I placed on the face of this earth to do?" I asked myself those questions while going through the darkest seasons of my life. I decided that I was going to turn my pain into purpose.

I have always known that I was put in this world for something bigger than myself—my God-given purpose. I went on a journey of self-discovery to identify my purpose. The enemy would not attack me so much unless there was a great calling on my life. I started to seek God more daily in regard to the purpose He had for my life. I slowed down, rested in Him, and worried less. I took some time every day to tune in to the Holy Spirit. I prayed, meditated, worshiped, and read the Word of God. I also invested in books and mentorship sessions and attended seminars.

Process For Purpose

In his book, *The Purpose Driven Life*, Pastor Rick Warren explains that knowing our purpose gives meaning to our lives. He stated that the purpose of our life is far greater than our own personal fulfilment, peace of mind, or happiness.

I went to God every day, asking Him to reveal the purpose that He had for my life. He would download things into my spirit or speak to me in dreams. I had a dream one morning, and in the dream, this girl was telling me that she was here to frustrate my purpose. I then realized that my destiny was being affected by the enemy. The devil came up against me with lies and other attacks because he was terrified of my God-given potential. He was trying to cut off my destiny before it could be fulfilled, but I already made up my mind that I was going to turn my pain into purpose.

Instead of sitting and waiting for circumstances to change, seek God and find out what He wants to do through you in the situation. The enemy attacks us mostly in the areas of our purpose through marital issues, finances, children or sickness, etc. These are mostly areas of ministry. I looked at the areas in my life where the enemy was fighting me the most and started to learn more about those areas. In doing so, I realized that there was this passion and drive that rose up in me to learn more about those areas.

I started to journal whatever I learned from the Holy Spirit. He would use me in the area I was having the most warfare in by allowing friends and family to call who had a similar situation that I was going through. I found myself
90

ministering to them and, in doing so, I was encouraged. I shared whatever the Holy Spirit dropped in my spirit and what I had learned. I have seen people get deliverance and get a hold of the truth and freedom in God. This gave me the drive to seek God's presence even more. I was getting a glimpse of what my purpose was and the purpose of the situation I was going through.

Your purpose will not come to you all at once. It is bigger and greater than you can imagine, and it takes time. Your specific purpose will not be clear to you at first, until God starts to reveal it to you. Finding and pursuing purpose is a lifelong journey. You must trust God and allow Him to lead you. As God starts to reveal your purpose in this season of your life, you will see your passion and uniqueness come alive. You will also see how well it fits into the kingdom of God. He has the roadmap for your life. He already had a plan for you before you were even formed in your mother's womb. It is not enough to know what your purpose is; you need to do something about it. To fulfill your life's purpose, you need to pursue it every day.

When I shifted my perspective from what I was going through and decided to find my purpose, I started to see my life shifting towards the purpose and plans God had for my life. Your storms can often feel like punishment, but they play an important role in shaping you into who you are called to be. Don't get distracted by how it looks; use the pressure to step into your purpose. Remain steadfast in the storm; your breakthrough is right around the corner.

Don't waste your pain. Let the enemy pay for all the heartache and pain you have gone through. Get up and push through your challenges despite the pain you are feeling. Take your focus off your situation and seek to help others who are going through a similar situation. God has something great for you to do as the person He wants you to be. The unexpected pain and circumstances that surface in our lives are an opportunity to become what He wants us to be and to do what He has called us to do.

Pursuing purpose requires faith, obedience, and knowing the promises of God. You can never fulfill God's purpose in your own strength; you have to appropriate the promises of God. Faith comes by hearing the Word of God. You must feed your spirit daily with the Word of God and listen to His leading.

Everything is purposeful; God has a purpose for your life. It doesn't matter what the odds are, He will bring all the right people and put all the right pieces together for that purpose to come to pass. Remember, all things will work out for your good, even the situations that seem so overwhelming, which cause you to feel like you are losing your mind. Nothing is working against you but for you. Pursue God and purpose, and you will see a shift in your perspective. I have learned to trust that God has the best plans for me, even when I don't always understand what is going on or why.

God Wastes Nothing

A thousand years is like one day in the courts of God (see 2 Peter 3:8). You may have been going through your situation for a long time and think you are getting old and your life seems wasted. God can restore those years in just one day. He's the God of restoration. He sees your tears, pain, and heartache, and those are not wasted to Him.

I have been going through my situation for quite some time without any breakthrough, but I choose not to let that place a hold on my life. From God's perspective, I don't see those years as wasted because I got married, had my daughter, and was able to stay home with her from birth until now. From my perspective, the years seemed wasted because my aim was to move on to my master's degree and rise to the top in my place of employment.

God has a plan for me despite how it happened and how it might look. My years are not wasted in His sight. Joseph's years may have seemed wasted in the natural world, but God was doing something spiritual. That is how it is with you and me. God is working with us through the years of our lives that seem stagnant and hopeless. God is a restorer and, just like Job, you are about to get double for all your wasted years. Be encouraged.

Be Purposeful And Deliberate In Your Pursuit Of God

Never stop pursuing God with all your heart. Make that your number one priority each day, and be intentional about doing so. When your relationship with God is in alignment, every other relationship will be in place. Without Him, we cannot complete what He has placed us on the face of the earth to do. Remember, He has the blueprint for our lives and knows the path our lives will take.

In the darkest seasons of my life, no education or success could give me the peace and strength that God gave me. I had to truly rely on Him because it was enough to make me lose my mind, but God! What I learned is that He really wants to have a relationship with us, and He is waiting for us to pursue it. The Bible says if we seek Him, we will find Him, if we seek with all our hearts (see Jeremiah 29:13). I sought after Him with everything I got, and I did find Him. I started to feel a peace like never before. My mind was not fearful of the unknown anymore because my mind was fixed on Him. I started to see life from His perspective. I became hopeful again and started to pursue purpose.

God is so strategic and purposeful that even the mess you are in can be used to bless you. Before this season of my life, I was doing life according to the norm of society—get an education, buy a house, and have children, but God had another plan for my life. He knows there is purpose in me and for Him to bring it to come to pass, He would have to

94

disrupt my life by any means to bring it to fulfilment. Yes, what I went through was very heart-wrenching; it tarnished my reputation in the natural. I would never choose to go through that if it was up to me, but God knows what He is doing, and I know He will get the glory from it.

If I didn't go through my experience, I would not have written this book. It was not in my mind to do nor did I plan to, but God! I always performed badly in English Language. It took me three attempts before I passed the subject. So, I didn't see myself as a writer. One day, after coming from a conference, I heard the Holy Spirit say, "Write." I started and I couldn't stop. When you yield to the process and allow Him to do His great work in you, then you will start to see purpose coming forth in your life. Allow Him to refine you. You are a diamond and must go through the refiner's fire in order for you to shine bright and do His great work. I am not going to tell you that I yielded immediately. I was merely existing, waiting for the court case to be over.

God didn't want me to merely exist; He wanted me to fulfill my purpose. I kept hearing about yielding to God, but to be honest, I didn't know how to. By being willing and allowing the Holy Spirit to lead me, I started to learn what it meant to yield to God and allow Him to steer the ship of my life. That was when I started to have a different mindset about my situation. I started to live on purpose instead of merely existing until the court case is over. I started to pursue God with all I have every day. I was intentional about it because

I was yearning for a change in my life so I could bring about a change in the lives of those around me.

Our processing can be very hard because it is stripping away and revealing things about ourselves that we didn't know was there; things we may not like. The process disrupts our comfort zone and pushes us out into the unknown, which is a bit scarier than what we are used to. The longer you take to yield, the harder and longer the processing will take. My processing was long, yet it felt short when I yielded and started living on purpose.

The race is not for the swift but for those who will endure to the end (see Ecclesiastes 9:11).

Be patient with yourself. Find your WHY and keep on going. When you have a WHY, it gives you more reasons to press on. Most people tend to abort their purpose in their season of waiting. Sometimes they give up when they are right at the edge of their breakthrough. Hold on a little longer. Stay anchored in the presence of God, even if you must hold on by a thread. Don't let go! Surround yourself with the right people—those who will encourage you in the process and cheer you on all the way.

Chapter 7

Persevere And Pass Your Test

---

1 Peter 4:12 - Beloved, think it not strange concerning the fiery trial which is to try you, as though some strange thing happened unto you. (KJV).

God wants us to pass our test so we can move on to the next level. Similar to the school system, you are not able to move to the next level if you don't complete the first level, unless you are exempt to move on with certain criteria. How is your attitude when going through your test? Are you murmuring and complaining, or is it one of learning and growth? I believe that our posture has a lot to do with whether we pass our test or not. It is not up to God; it is up to us to choose the right posture. Not all tests are easy and equal; some you must retake in order to pass them.

The test is used to refine our character and bring out what we have on the inside of us. Hebrews 12:11 says it all: **"Now no chastening for the present seemeth to be joyous, but grievous: nevertheless afterward it yieldeth the peaceable fruit of righteousness unto them which are**

exercised thereby." (KJV). Our test may not be easy, but it will be worth it in the end, once we pass it.

I have learned that it is better to pass the test on the first try than to keep repeating the same test. Jesus passed His test when He was tempted in the wilderness by the devil, and we can too. Jesus used the Word of God to pass His test, and so should we. Learn the Word of God and use it as a weapon and armour in your test. It is our greatest tool that is needed to pass our test of life. As believers, we need to be thoroughly equipped according to 2 Timothy 3:17. Hebrews 4:12 says the word is **"… living and powerful, and sharper than any two-edged sword…" (NKJV).** Use it like Jesus did to defeat the devil.

You won't move to the next level until you pass that test. So, the next time someone cuts you off in traffic, instead of cursing and getting angry, breathe a word of prayer. If someone makes a rude comment about you, instead of thinking about repaying that person with evil, pray for them. Instead of becoming impatient, practice patience. Don't keep responding in the old way and expect to pass your test. Do what the Word of God says in regard to the situation, and watch God work in your life. Pass your test; your next level is waiting on you; there are lives to be impacted.

Live Above Your Circumstances

We often allow our circumstances to stop us from truly living our lives. Life happens, and we must face that reality.

We are living in a fallen world. We must learn to live above our circumstances no matter how bad they are. It is the will of God for us to have joy and enjoy every stage of our lives whether good or bad. Joy is a fruit of the Spirit, and as a child of God, joy should be evident in our lives despite what we are going through.

Don't wait for your circumstances to come to an end; find joy while going through it. It is not what you go through but how you go through it. Life goes on; live and enjoy every moment of your life. Take it one day at a time with the help of God. Try to find the beauty in what you are going through; you still have life. You may never know what can happen tomorrow, so learn to dance in your storm. Practice gratitude daily. Pay attention to your most dominant thoughts because they create your emotions.

I have learned to live through my storm. I could have chosen to wait until my case was over to get married, have a child, pursue studies, and even write this book. No, I chose the opposite, despite what I was going through by the grace of God. I am going to push for all that God has for me and not wait until I am in a better position. The thing is, time waits on no man. God is our source, and He uses resources to bless us. With His strength, I decided that whatever He tells me to do, I am going to move by faith. He will make a way when He sees my faith.

You won't get up every day and feel like living above your circumstances, but you must be intentional about doing so.

Life is beautiful despite the wickedness that has been taking place. We don't need a whole lot of material things to enjoy life; simple things are blessings. Live, laugh, and love. Find beauty in everyday life, even if you must look a little harder.

Practice Daily Affirmations

I am big on affirmations because I have seen it work in my life, especially in my emotions. Daily we tend to encounter a lot of negative thoughts running endlessly through our minds. Daily affirmations can help to rewire our brains, build our self-esteem, and change those negative thought patterns. Think about what you are thinking about because if you don't, those negative thoughts will have a field day in your mind and on your emotions. I realised that whenever I was feeling down and discouraged, it was because of the thoughts playing in my mind at the moment.

Keep an inventory of your thoughts, and whenever those negative thoughts come, replace them with positive ones. Proverbs 18:21 says death and life are in the power of the tongue, and those who love it will eat its fruit. What are you speaking over your life and into your situation? Are they faith-filled words? Are you agreeing with God or your situation?

You may be going through a hard time right now, but you are not what you are going through. Don't let it define you.

∂   You are who God says you are.

- ∂ You are more than a conqueror.
- ∂ You are blessed and favoured.
- ∂ You are victorious.
- ∂ You are capable.
- ∂ You are the head and not the tail.
- ∂ You are above and not beneath.
- ∂ You are resilient.
- ∂ You are strong.
- ∂ You are loved.
- ∂ You are unstoppable.
- ∂ You are chosen.

Choose to speak life into your situation until what you are speaking manifests. Our words are powerful, and they frame our reality.

Agree with God and speak what you want to see come to pass in your life despite the negatives and setbacks. Audibly confessing God's Word is a life-changing practice for me. It gives me a sense of hope and peace. It helps me to visualise what I want to see come to pass in my life. Make it a habit to examine the thoughts racing through your mind and the words coming out of your mouth. Be intentional about what you hear, think, and speak because you are setting the stage for your reality. Begin today and every day; speak positive, faith-filled words over your life. Speak things that line up with God's Word and what it says about you, not what your feelings, circumstances, or other people might tell you.

Learn To Encourage Yourself

Have you ever been at a place where God was sending words for everyone except you? I have been there. I was longing for a word of encouragement or a prophecy, something to know that God hadn't forgotten about me. Like David, we need to learn to encourage ourselves. 1 Samuel 30:6 says David was greatly distressed because the men were talking about stoning him, but David strengthened himself in the Lord, his God. At his lowest point, David sought God for strength.

Life is unpredictable, and there are times when we are hit by circumstances that we didn't see coming. I would never think in a million years that I would end up in jail. That is the time to find encouragement in the Lord. I was frightened with no one to help me in that prison cell, so I leaned on the Lord for strength. There will come a point in your situation when you need a word of encouragement, and no one will be there to encourage you or understand your feelings. You must learn to encourage yourself in God; speak over yourself. Remind yourself that "this too shall pass." Weeping may endure for a night, but joy comes in the morning (see Psalm 30:5).

Discouragement is as real as it can be. I have been there where all I needed was a word of encouragement in my season for what I was going through. I had to find encouragement from the Word of God or a song that was downloaded in my spirit. Your pastor, minister, or church sister will not always be around in your lowest when all you need is a word of encouragement. Learn to encourage yourself in the Lord. Don't stay in your state of discouragement. Shake it off and allow the Spirit of God to speak encouragement to your spirit. You may be in the valley now but don't stay in the valley. There is light at the end of the tunnel; look for the spark and keep on going. God's got you! He will never leave or forsake you.

Joy Is Possible In Your Test

Nehemiah 8:10 - Then he said unto them, Go your way, eat the fat, and drink the sweet, and send portions unto them for whom nothing is prepared: for this day is holy unto our Lord: neither be ye sorry; for the joy of the Lord is your strength. (KJV).

Joy is possible when going through your testing and trials if you don't allow the situation to get inside of you and cause bitterness. It is not what is on the outside of the boat that causes the boat to sink, but what is on the inside. You are not going to wake up every day feeling joyful, but you can choose to be joyful. It is a choice!

My situation has given me many reasons to walk around in self-pity and bitterness, but I choose to think of the goodness and mercy of God. I choose to be better and not bitter. I have a lot to be thankful for despite my situation. I have many things that other people wish they had. Joy is an inside feeling that is not predicated on things or people. Joy is naturally generated. When you have the joy of the Lord, no external circumstances can cause you to lose hope. God gives joy even in the midst of chaos and confusion; God gives calmness. Joy is always available to us when we remain in Christ, in spite of what life may throw at us. Who are you leaning on for your joy?

I am joyful when I see my daughter growing up before my eyes. I am grateful to be able to stay with her from birth until now. She brings me a lot of joy. My husband is my number one cheerleader and supporter, and that causes my heart to burst with joy. My family, friends, reading my Bible, encouraging others, going to church, and my church community are all sources of joy. I could go on and on, but you get the picture. Despite what you are going through, choose to find the things in life that bring you joy and focus on them.

Life is beautiful no matter how terrible the world we are living in might seem. Joy should be evident in our lives as a child of God. James 1:2-4 says, **"My brethren, count it all joy when ye fall into divers temptations; Knowing this, that the trying of your faith worketh patience. But let patience have her perfect work, that ye may be perfect and entire, wanting nothing." (KJV).** How do we count it all joy? By learning from it and allowing God to do His good work in you so you can come through as pure gold for your next level. There is a testimony in your trial.

True joy does not stem from our circumstances but from our trust and relationship with Jesus through the Holy Spirit.

Don't Just Go Through It, Grow Through It

God uses difficulties, inconveniences, and delays to do a work in us. Don't just sit down and let life pass you by because you are waiting for a particular season of your life to come to an end. Instead, take life one day at a time by doing what you can control in the situation. Remember, we are only given one life to live, and our Creator expects us to live it fully. What do you have in the now of that season that can prepare you for where you want to go in life? Your next is connected to your now. Getting up each day whining and complaining will not allow you to grow. That will only cause you to become bitter and miserable.

I have learned to grow through what I am going through. I use my time wisely to develop areas of my life that need to be worked on for the next season of my life where God wants to take me. I realised that sitting down and playing a victim would not allow me to grow but would keep me stuck in a prison of bitterness, misery, anger, and unforgiveness.

Growth is not easy or comfortable, but it is necessary and takes a made-up mind with intentionality. Growth is painful because you are stretched beyond your comfort zone. It can be likened to being crushed like an olive to extract the oil from it. Without that olive being crushed, there won't be any oil. If we are not pushed to grow, we will remain stuck, and the gifting and calling on our lives will not be pulled out from within us. With the stretching I went through, I had to learn how to pull on Jesus with everything I had inside of me.

Sometimes God disrupts our lives, so we don't remain in the same place. We can get so comfortable in our little box because it is all we know. We wait for things to get better when God is saying move. With God, you don't see to go; you need to go to see. So, what if He doesn't tell you what the outcome will look like? God is good. Whatever He does with your life is good. You might not see and understand it now, but it is good. This is no time to complain about things getting worse; go and grow. You will not have the revelation for the next phase of your life until you move in this phase. Don't die there; make that move. There is more awaiting you on the other side of growth.

Life may seem unfair, and you don't understand it. Don't just go through it, grow through it. My situation was unfair, and I didn't understand it, but I leaned on His understanding and not my own. Sometimes we are in too much of a hurry to come out of our situation that we don't see the opportunity to grow while in it. There are so many hidden lessons in our pain, but because we don't stop to learn or listen, we miss the opportunity it brings to grow. I have reached a point in my circumstances where I decided not to let it cause me to become the victim anymore, and whatever I can learn along the journey, I am willing to.

Chapter 8

God Is A Restorer

Joel 2:25 - And I will restore to you the years that the locust hath eaten, the cankerworm, and the caterpiller, and the palmerworm, my great army which I sent among you. (KJV).

I hold this scripture dear to my heart because I know God honours His Word. When I read a promise in the Bible, I hold it in my heart. I attach my faith to what God has said. Once He says it, He will do it. I may not know how, when, where, and who He might use, but I know He is going to do it. It doesn't matter how many years or how much you have lost, God will restore.

I always like to use Job as my encouragement. Job lost all his children along with his wealth and possessions in just one day. Despite his suffering, Job remained and trusted God's will for his life. In Job 42, God restored all that Job lost in double portions. God wants to do the same for you and me, but we must trust Him and remain faithful in the test.

You may ask, "What about the opportunities I have missed?" or "What about the time I have wasted?" Whatever life has taken from you, God can restore. You may not get exactly what you want, but He will give you what is best. What is gone is gone, so focus on the new that God has in store for you. What I realized is that God has my best interest at heart. My best is the smallest in His sight, and He wants to give me bigger and better. But to receive it, I have to let go of the past and allow Him to prepare me for the future. Sometimes we are so blinded by the situation that we can't fathom how God is going to replace what we have lost. Remember, He doesn't take and not replace it with better, so dry your tears, remove the frown from your face, and brush off your worries. God is still in the restoration business!

I experienced restoration in my health when no doctor could tell me what was happening in my body. My spiritual life was restored. My peace of mind and strength was restored as well. I have been experiencing restoration despite my situation because I continue to remain faithful and trust God. The experience was rough, but think of the things you have learned while going through your process. The challenges did not come to kill you; they are there to mature you into the person God wants you to be. Your life or situation is never beyond repair. God is a God of restoration. I am looking forward to all that I have lost being restored doublefold, but until then, I will continue to be faithful and trust God.

Can I report that in July 2023, I stepped out in faith with no steady income and started my master's degree with the help of God. Listen, God is a provider. All He needs is your faith coupled with your actions behind it. To God be all the glory.

Life Of A Seed: Choose To Be Planted, Not Buried

Psalm 1:3 - And he shall be like a tree planted by the rivers of water, that bringeth forth his fruit in his season; his leaf also shall not wither; and whatsoever he doeth shall prosper. (KJV).

For a seed to grow, you must first plant it in the ground and bury it with dirt so it can begin germination. According to the Oxford Dictionary, germination is the development of a plant from a seed or the process of something coming into existence. First, the seed must be planted in the right environment for it to grow.

Sometimes we go through seasons in life where we feel like nothing is happening in our lives; we feel stuck, and nothing is moving. That is the time when God is building deep roots within us. That is the time our character, integrity, patience, and humility are being developed. God has you in this place not to punish you but to build your roots. He does the work from within because out of the abundance of the heart, the mouth speaks (see Matthew 12:34). So, He has to first deal with those things on the inside that need to be pulled to the surface.

We can easily get frustrated with the process of being planted, but if we change our perspective and remember that God says in His Word that all things work together for good to those who are called according to His purpose, then we will start looking at our circumstances in another light. Planting is only for a season. When He knows you are ready, He will allow you to bring forth fruit in that season. I know the feeling of being planted for a long time and waiting for your season to come; I have been there.

Pain in life is inevitable. We will go through some things in our lives. We are a seed with fruit inside of us, and for God to use us effectively, we need to be pruned. For a tree to be pruned, it must be planted in the ground and nurtured for it to spring forth and bear fruit in its season.

A seed takes time to grow. It can be buried in the ground for weeks without any noticeable change. The fact that we don't see the seed doesn't mean it is not there. Sometimes we pray and declare a thing and then lose patience because it doesn't manifest right away. Because you are planted, you will germinate and bear fruit.

The devil didn't know that when he decided to put you underneath the earth, he wasn't really burying you; he was preparing you to grow and bear fruit. Tell the devil you are a seed! You will spring forth and bloom like never before.

Bloom where you are planted. It doesn't matter where a seed is planted, it just needs the right conditions to grow into that tree and bear fruit. That is how it should be with us; it doesn't matter what our circumstances are, it shouldn't stop us from blooming into the fruit-bearing tree that we were created to be. Flourish and thrive, despite how bad the circumstances may seem.

Due Season

Ecclesiastes 3:1 - To every thing there is a season, and a time to every purpose under the heaven: (KJV).

We have a due season for whatever situation we may be facing. One of the hardest things to do is to keep persevering when there is no evidence that what we are believing for will come to pass. Some seasons can be longer than others, but it doesn't matter how long it takes, it will come to an end when God says so. As for my court case, I know there is a due season when everything will turn in my favour and for the glory of God. Yes, I speak with confidence because of the God I serve. He has never lost a battle, so that is where I place my hope and confidence. As stated in Ecclesiastes, everything under the sun has an appointed time. Even your suffering and pain have a due season for when they will end.

You may be stuck in a cycle in your life with no end in sight, but your due season is coming when you least expect it. Due season means there is a set time for your breakthrough, a set time for that thing you have been praying for to manifest in your life, so continue to be faithful and persevere. The enemy will not have the final say. When it is due, there is nothing no one can do to stop it.

Galatians 6:9 - And let us not be weary in well doing: for in due season we shall reap, if we faint not. (KJV).

There is a due season if we faint not. There is seedtime, and there is also harvest time; your harvest time is coming, so don't faint, and don't get weary or lose heart.

Don't quit. Your due season might just be right around the corner. Some people quit too soon and miss their due season. If you can make it through one season, you will be able to embrace the next. If you can make it through your season of sickness, God will bring you into a season of perfect health. If you can make it through the season of lack, God will bring you into a season of abundance. If you can make it through the season of loneliness, God will bring you to a season of companionship. If you can endure this season of childlessness, God will open your womb like Hannah and give you a Samuel. Don't be disheartened. Don't be discouraged, and don't grow weary. No matter the season you are in right now, persevere through it so you can get to your due season.

God will strengthen you and give you hope. Stay in the good fight of faith. Stay prayerful, obedient, willing, and faithful to God. Trust in His goodness and love. Every trial has an expiry date, and your time and season have a due date. Our God is a faithful restorer, and His plan never changes. Press into the things of God with all you got; you will reap. What God promised you then is still available to you. Your due season is almost here. Don't faint! Keep a good attitude and do the right thing even when it is hard. Be encouraged because your appointed time of increase, blessing, favour, and promotion is on its way, and God will fulfill every dream and desire He placed inside you.

Trust God's Track Record

Numbers 23:19 - God is not a man, that he should lie; neither the son of man, that he should repent: hath he said, and shall he not do it? or hath he spoken, and shall he not make it good? (KJV).

If God did it before, He can surely do it again. God is the same yesterday, today, and forever (see Hebrews 13:8). God is faithful and cannot fail. He cannot lie. He is the all-powerful and all-knowing God, so there is nothing in this world He cannot do. Yes, the situation may seem big and the wait long, but nothing is too hard for God to do. We tend to limit God because He didn't work on our timetable or according to how we expect Him to.

Let me remind you that God parted the Red Sea for the children of Israel, restored sight to the blind, cast out demons, healed the sick, and caused Sarah to conceive when she was ninety-nine years old. When He speaks, winds and waves must obey. I could go on and on. Has He ever made a promise and not carried it out? Has He done it before and is unable to do it again? God doesn't lie. We lie. He doesn't change His mind. We change our minds all the time. God isn't human. We are human and can be limited. God is a promise keeper. We break a lot of promises. God speaks, and it happens. When we speak, it may or may not happen.

Let me encourage you to take a moment today and reflect on God's goodness, grace, and mercy towards us. In spite of ourselves and our circumstances, He has never left or forsaken us. When we were sick, He is a healer. When we are in need, He provides. When we are in need of comfort, He comforts us. It doesn't matter what you are going through and how long you have been going through it, God will come through for you at the right time.

Get excited because what He did before, He can surely do it again. He doesn't just perform the miracle one time and is unable to do it again. I have learned to trust His track record because He has come through so many times for me in my situations. Whenever I pray, He always sends help right on time, when I need it the most. I know it is hard to fathom how God is going to work things out when you are in the midst of your situation, but if He restored you before, He is able to do it again. If He blessed you before, He is able to bless you again. If He opened doors of opportunity before, He can do it again. We serve an unlimited God. He didn't promise to bless you once and that was it.

Hold on to what God has done already; don't limit Him because of your situation. Once God says it, He will do it.

There is nothing or no one who can stop the blessings of God in your life. Start living by what you know. You know God has a great plan for your life. You know He is the God of exceedingly abundantly above all that you ask or think (see Ephesians 3:20). Shake off those feelings of discouragement and disappointment. Fix your eyes on God and not your situation; the victory is already won. Trust God's track record.

Arise And Shine, Your Time Has Come

Isaiah 60:1 - Arise, shine; for thy light is come, and the glory of the Lord is risen upon thee. (KJV).

It is time to bounce back. It is time to arise and shine for your time has come. Get up, dry those tears, and shake off self-pity. Square your shoulders, stand tall, look that situation in the face, and let it know that you serve a big God who is not constrained by time or seasons. Despite your situation, you can testify of God's grace, strength, and provisions. There were days when you felt like He was going to come through for you, and He did. God sustained you and gave you the power to bounce right back, to start feeling alive and ready to conquer what may come your way again. I am a living witness to that kind of experience, and I thank God for the strength and ability to rise again. Is it always easy? Absolutely not! But it is doable with God's help and strength. I have days when I felt drained and ready to throw in the towel, but God would not allow it. He would say, "No, My child. There is more in you than what meets the eye.

115

Continue to push." I didn't know my strength until I stumbled upon it by the grace of God.

Don't allow your situation to keep you down. See beyond what you are going through, even if you must crawl to get there; don't stay there. The world is waiting for you to make an impact. Fight through those tears, discouragement, disappointments, and setbacks. Persevere; you are building your faith muscle. I had my fair share of pity parties and have decided that I am no longer living there. It is time to arise and yield and allow God to make new wine out of me. Let me encourage you as I continue to encourage myself. Life will always have ups and downs. Some days, you will feel like you can conquer the world or you are on top of the world; other days, you will wonder, "Where is God? Can't He see that I'm hurting?" Don't fear or be dismayed; God is still there. You may not know how, when, or where, but He will give you the grace, strength, and power to arise and shine.

Don't Be Afraid

2 Timothy 1:7 says God has not given us a spirit of fear, but of power, love, and a sound mind. God has commanded us so many times in scripture not to be afraid. Fear can cripple you. I was there when I experienced unknown health challenges. I was fearful that every day would be my last day. I would be afraid to be alone, travel alone, fearful that I might not get to see my daughter growing up. Fear crippled

and robbed me of my peace of mind and joy every day. Fear is a spirit; that is what it states in 2 Timothy 1:7.

Back in 2017, when I was arrested, I became so fearful of seeing Fridays because it would take me back to that Friday when I was arrested. I was so fearful of the unknown. I felt like my life would get stuck in that phase forever like the others who had gone through the same thing. Life is so full of the unknown, which can cause us to panic and ask a lot of questions. Fear can become our constant companion and rob us of our joy if we don't evict it from the room. Did you know that you can be going to church and still be living in fear? It happens to the best of us no matter how strong we think we are.

Use the Word of God to fight your fear. It works. I had to find scriptures, speak them over my life, and meditate on them. That was how I was able to stop living in crippling fear. Yes, it still comes back to check me from time to time, but I have the Word of God in my heart to remind me that fear is not of Him. I have learned to take my thoughts captive and bring them under the subjection of God. Fear starts in your mind, so if you can take those negative thoughts captive, you can have dominion over fear. I have also learned to do it afraid. When I feel fearful to step out and do something that the Lord has impressed on me, and those negative thoughts come rushing in, I would just step out anyway with my heart racing, knees wobbling, and hands trembling. Listen, we have to move despite our fear because if we don't, we will stay stuck in that same position forever.

As the quote states, "Everything you want is on the other side of fear." Don't allow fear to keep you down. When fear rises its ugly head, remember you can do all things through Christ who gives you strength (see Philippians 4:13). If it is sickness in your body and you constantly fear that you are going to die, remember the Word of God says you shall not die but live to declare the Word of God (see Psalm 118:17). You might be afraid of the unknown, remember God has a plan for your life and it is to prosper you and not to harm you but bring you hope and a future (see Jeremiah 29:11). Don't live constantly in fear; it is not the will of God for you. According to John 10:10, He came that we might have life and life more abundantly. Surrender your fears to God and allow Him to deliver and heal your heart from that spirit of fear. Always choose faith over fear.

Lessons Learned In The Process

I have learned to appreciate my process despite how hard and lonely it can feel. I have learned that I was never alone. God is with me all the way, even when I feel alone. Like David said, "It was good that I was afflicted." (see Psalm 119:71). How can we say that God is a provider if we have not gone through a situation where we had to rely on Him to provide? We know Him as Healer because we have been afflicted in the body. All that we have been through, or are going through, are testimonies that others are waiting on to be delivered from their circumstances. Without a test, there will be no testimony; your story is bigger than you.

I used to hear people talk about how God brought them through some serious circumstances in their lives, but I had never experienced that for myself. I am truly grateful to have my own testimony regardless of how it happened. When circumstances and situations arise, I can always remember what He had brought me through.

There are days you must tell yourself that all things are working for your good, even when it does not look or feel good. Oh, I have to tell myself that every time I go to court, especially when my case is being constantly delayed without any logical reason. You must tell yourself that by His stripes, you are healed, even when the symptoms are overbearing and your body isn't lining up with the Word of God about healing. Like Ezekiel, we must continually speak to the dry bones until life comes about.

Our words are powerful and set the pace for our breakthrough. I have learned that we must see it before it happens and wrap our faith around it. In the natural, it is seeing before believing, but in the spiritual, it is believing before seeing. As the scripture says, we walk by faith and not sight (see 2 Corinthians 5:7). The just live by faith. God is not a respecter of persons. He sends the rain on the just and unjust. Being a Christian doesn't mean we will never face trials and tribulations; that is where some Christians get it wrong and shy away from their processing. When God wants to bring forth new wine in you, He cannot pour it on old wine or it will become contaminated. Let God process you; He knows what He is doing.

I may never understand why I am going through what I am going through, but I know that God has a greater purpose and plan for my life. He will manifest it little by little. I am an encourager at heart; I love to encourage people, and I find myself helping people more while I am going through my own storm. One day I asked God, "How can I encourage people when I have been going through my own storm for years now? Don't You think people are going to ask, 'Where is your God? Why hasn't He delivered you?'" The Holy Spirit told me not to worry about that and just allow myself to be used as a vessel despite my circumstances.

I felt unworthy and discouraged and didn't want to share what I was going through. God constantly reminded me that my story is for His glory. I wanted this season to end before writing this book, but God would have it otherwise. He wanted me to share what I am going through and how I deal with it to help others.

God is not bound by your situation. He can use you, even while you are going through it, but you must yield and allow Him to use you. You may not see yourself as significant—as I did—until you allow Him to have His way in your life. I am not there yet, but I am allowing Him to order my steps each day of my life.

I have also learned the true meaning of life and what really matters. Most of the things we are running after are of no true lasting value. Our true fulfilment is found in Christ, when we are walking in the purpose He has for our lives.

There is purpose in your pain. God is not a cruel Father who wants to see us suffer while He sits back and does nothing. He promised us that despite how bad our situation might look, He will work it out for our good.

Waiting is a process that we must go through at some point in our lives, whether in the natural or spiritual, but it is our posture of waiting that will determine if we win or lose. I know waiting is not easy when you are in a situation and need an answer now.

Hold On! Don't Give Up In The Process

Hang tight! Your breakthrough is right around the corner. It could be today or tomorrow; you may not know. Don't throw in the towel. Some people give up on the brink of their breakthrough. Stay the course. God will come through for you. It doesn't matter how long your breakthrough is taking, it is on its way. Remember, our God is a God of the *suddenly*.

You may feel stuck; your prayers seem fruitless, and you feel like giving up. I have been there a few times, but God would not allow me to give up because He knows there is greatness inside me waiting to be birthed. If we can hold on a bit longer, we will see the results of our prayers, praise, and worship; then we will know that they were not in vain.

I ask God daily for inner strength to keep me going until my time of breakthrough because I cannot do it all by myself. If it was up to me and my strength alone, I would have given up a long time ago. His strength is perfect in our weakness (see 2 Corinthians 12:9), so rely on Him for strength.

It has been six years and four months at the writing of this book since I have been waiting for this court matter to come to an end. I realized that great people of faith in the Bible had to wait a while for their breakthrough, so I am counted among the great if God is allowing me to wait this long.

There was a lady with an issue of blood for twelve years. One encounter with Jesus by just touching the hem of His garment and she was healed. Continue to touch God with your prayers, praise, and worship. You may just be a prayer, praise, and worship away from your breakthrough. While you wait, allow God to be the focus and not your situation. You will find yourself getting stronger with each passing day. I honestly didn't believe I could have lasted a year, much less years.

Don't give in. Stay on the Potter's wheel and allow Him to mold and make you. The Potter knows best. If it wasn't for prayer and practicing the presence of God, I would not have made it this far. The presence of God is so real. Seek intimacy with Him and allow Him to work in you. I don't know why my breakthrough is taking so long, but what I know is that God is my source of strength and comfort. He can become yours too, if you allow Him to.

Every day is a choice for me. I choose to trust God. I choose to continue in fasting, prayer, worship, and continual reading of my Bible. I choose to hold dear to His promises. Just because I don't understand doesn't change who God is.

Don't allow your situation to define the rest of your life. Climb over that obstacle and continue moving forward. He hasn't brought you this far to leave you. He is a God of completion. I refuse to believe that He brought me this far to leave me. God is faithful; He will come through for us. Our victory is sure in Him. I am feeling so encouraged as I am encouraging you. Don't let this become your final destination. Keep believing God's promises above your situation, and continue to be faithful. Don't quit! The delay is not denial. God is still working on you; wait patiently on His timing. God doesn't want you to quit!

About the Author

Sherine Leslie-Gooden is a compassionate servant of God with a passion to touch lives for the glory of God. She is married with a beautiful daughter. She is a graduate of the University of Technology Jamaica and is currently pursuing her master's degree in public administration. She is passionate about empowering and encouraging others to walk in their divine purpose despite the many obstacles and setbacks that may come their way. She lives by the motto, "Nothing is working against me; God will work it out for my good." Her favourite scripture is "And we know that all things work together for good to them that love God, to them who are the called according to his purpose." (Romans 8:28 - KJV).

www.ingramcontent.com/pod-product-compliance
Lightning Source LLC
Chambersburg PA
CBHW071835090426
42737CB00012B/2252